The

Growing in Kingdom Character

The Bible Teacher's Guide

Gregory Brown

Copyright © 2017, 2018 (2nd Edition) Gregory Brown

Unless otherwise noted, the primary Scriptures used are taken from the NET Bible ® copyright © 1996-2016 by Biblical Studies Press, L.L.C. All rights reserved.

Holy Bible, New International Version ®, NIV® Copyright © 1973, 1978, 1984 by Biblica, Inc.® Used by permission. All rights reserved worldwide.

Scripture quotations marked (ESV) are from The Holy Bible, English Standard Version® (ESV®) Copyright © 2001 by Crossway, a publishing ministry of Good News Publishers. All rights reserved.

Scripture quotations marked (NLT) are taken from the Holy Bible, New Living Translation, Copyright © 1996, 2004, 2007 by Tyndale House Foundation. Used by permission of Tyndale House Publishers, Inc., Carol Stream, Illinois 60188. All rights reserved.

Scripture quotations marked (NASB) are taken from the New American Standard Bible®, Copyright © 1960, 1962, 1963, 1968, 1971, 1972, 1973, 1975, 1977, and 1995 by The Lockman Foundation. Used by permission.

Scripture quotations marked (KJV) are from the King James Version of the Bible.

All emphases in Scripture quotations have been added.

BTG Publishing all rights reserved.

Endorsements

"*The Bible Teacher's Guide* ... will help any teacher study and get a better background for his/her Bible lessons. In addition, it will give direction and scope to teaching of the Word of God. Praise God for this contemporary introduction to the Word of God."

—Dr. Elmer Towns
Co-founder of Liberty University
Former Dean, Liberty Baptist Theological Seminary

"Expositional, theological, and candidly practical! I highly recommend The Bible Teacher's Guide for anyone seeking to better understand or teach God's Word."

—Dr. Young–Gil Kim
Founding President, Handong Global University

"Helpful to both the layman and the serious student, The Bible Teacher's Guide, by Dr. Greg Brown, is outstanding!"

—Dr. Neal Weaver
President, Louisiana Baptist University

"Whether you are preparing a Bible study, a sermon, or simply wanting to dive deeper into a personal study of God's Word, these will be very helpful tools."

—Eddie Byun
Missions and Teaching Pastor, Venture Christian Church, Los Gatos, California
Author of Justice Awakening

"I am happy that Greg is making his insights into God's truth available to a wider audience through these books. They bear the hallmarks of good Bible teaching: the result of rigorous Bible study and thoroughgoing application to the lives of people."

—Ajith Fernando
Teaching Director, Youth for Christ
Author of A Call to Joy and Pain

"The content of the series is rich. My prayer is that God will use it to help the body of Christ grow strong."

—Dr. Min Chung
Senior Pastor, Covenant Fellowship Church, Urbana, Illinois
Adjunct Professor, Urbana Theological Seminary

"Knowing the right questions to ask and how to go about answering them is fundamental to learning in any subject matter. Greg demonstrates this convincingly."

—Dr. William Moulder
Professor of Biblical Studies, Trinity International University

"Pastor Greg is passionate about the Word of God, rigorous and thorough in his approach to the study of it... I am pleased to recommend The Bible Teacher's Guide to anyone who hungers for the living Word."

—Dr. JunMo Cho
Professor of Linguistics, Handong Global University
Contemporary Christian Music Recording Artist

"I can't imagine any student of Scripture not benefiting by this work."

—Steven J. Cole
Pastor, Flagstaff Christian Fellowship, Flagstaff, Arizona
Author of the Riches from the Word series

Contents

Preface...11
Introduction...13
Blessed Are the Poor in Spirit...15
Blessed Are the Mourners...29
Blessed Are the Meek...43
Blessed Are the Hungry...57
Blessed Are the Merciful...71
Blessed Are the Pure in Heart...85
Blessed Are the Peacemakers...97
Blessed Are the Persecuted...109
Appendix 1: Study Group Tips...119
Appendix 2: Reflection Questions...121
Appendix 3: Walking the Romans Road...123
Coming Soon...129
About the Author...131
Notes...133

Preface

And entrust what you heard me say in the presence of
many others as witnesses to faithful people
2 Timothy 2:2 (NET)

Paul's words to Timothy still apply to us today. The church needs teachers who clearly and fearlessly teach the Word of God. With this in mind, The Bible Teacher's Guide (BTG) series was created. This series includes both expositional and topical studies, with resources to help teachers lead small groups, pastors prepare sermons, and individuals increase their knowledge of God's Word.

Each lesson is based around the hermeneutical principle that the original authors wrote in a similar manner as we do today—with the intention of being understood. Each paragraph and chapter of Scripture centers around one main thought, often called the Big Idea. After finding the Big Idea for each passage studied, students will discuss the Big Question, which will lead the small group (if applicable) through the entire text. Alongside the Big Question, note the added Observation, Interpretation, and Application Questions. The Observation Questions point out pivotal aspects of the text. The Interpretation Questions facilitate understanding through use of the context and other Scripture. The Application Questions lead to life principles coming out of the text. Not all questions will be used, but they have been given to help guide the teacher in preparing the lesson.

As the purpose of this guide is to make preparation easier for the teacher and study easier for the individual, many commentaries and sermons have been accessed in the development of each lesson. After meditating on the Scripture text and the lesson, the small group leader may wish to follow the suggested teaching outline:

1. Introduce the text and present the Big Question.
2. Allow several minutes for the members to discuss the question, search for the answers within the text, and listen to God speak to them through His Word.
3. Discuss the initial findings, then lead the group through the Observation, Interpretation, and Application Questions.

On the other hand, the leader may prefer to teach the lesson in part or in whole, and then give the Application Questions. He may also choose to use a "study group" method, where each member prepares beforehand and shares teaching responsibility (see Appendices 1 and 2). Some leaders may find it most effective to first read the main section of the lesson corporately, then to follow with a brief discussion of the topic and an Application Question.

Again, The Bible Teacher's Guide can be used as a manual to follow in teaching, a resource to use in preparation for teaching or preaching, or simply as an expositional devotional to enrich your own study. I pray that the Lord may bless your study, preparation, and teaching, and that in all of it you will find the fruit of the Holy Spirit abounding in your own life and in the lives of those you instruct.

Introduction

How can we grow in kingdom character?

When Christ came into the world, he preached the kingdom of heaven (Matt 4:17). He taught that not only was the kingdom something future but a present reality, as the kingdom of heaven was in their midst (Lk 17:21). The kingdom consists of all those who profess Christ as Lord—though all who profess are not truly saved (cf. Matt 7:21-23, 13:36-43). In Matthew 5:3-10, Christ introduces the character of those who are truly part of his kingdom. They are the poor in spirit, the mourners, the meek, and those who hunger and thirst for righteousness. They are the merciful, the pure in heart, the peacemakers, and those who are persecuted for righteousness. These character traits are affectionately called the Beatitudes, as each one begins with "Blessed" and finishes with a promise of God. If these characteristics are not in our lives, at least imperfectly, we are not truly part of Christ's kingdom.

However, the Beatitudes not only represent the nature of kingdom citizens, they also represent the aspirations of them. Only Christ perfectly modeled these characteristics, but each kingdom citizen should constantly aim to grow in them. As we consider the Beatitudes, they will both affirm if we have truly entered God's kingdom and also challenge us to grow in these kingdom characteristics. Lord, allow your kingdom to grow deep in us. Let your kingdom fill the whole earth at the King's coming. Lord, come! Lord, come! Amen.

Blessed Are the Poor in Spirit

When he saw the crowds, he went up the mountain. After he sat down his disciples came to him. Then he began to teach them by saying: "Blessed are the poor in spirit, for the kingdom of heaven belongs to them.
Matthew 5:1-3 (NET)

Interpretation Question: What is the Sermon on the Mount and what is its purpose?

In Matthew 5-7, Christ begins his Sermon on the Mount. This sermon takes only about ten minutes to read; however, many believe the original sermon was probably very long—possibly a couple of hours.[1] What we have in the Sermon on the Mount is most likely a summary of his teaching. In Luke 6, we see a similar but shorter sermon, except it's given on a plain instead of a mountain. Therefore, it's quite possible that this was a standard sermon that Christ preached wherever he went—a staple of his itinerant preaching.[2]

The background to the Sermon on the Mount is Christ's teaching and healing ministry in Galilee (cf. Matt 4:18-25). Because of this, his popularity had risen and crowds were flocking to him. He goes up on a mountain, sits down (the customary teaching posture of rabbis) and begins to preach to his disciples.[3]

The major theme of the Sermon on the Mount is the character of those in God's kingdom. Christ said this in Matthew 5:20, "For I tell you, unless your righteousness goes beyond that of the experts in the law and the Pharisees, you will never enter the kingdom of heaven." The Pharisees had a legalistic, external righteousness, but the righteousness Christ described was primarily of the heart. It is humble and not prideful like the Pharisees who did their righteous deeds to be seen by men (Matt 6:1-3). It is gentle in response to personal wrong, as Christ taught his followers to turn the other cheek (Matt 5:38-42). It is concerned with building up riches in heaven instead of building up riches on the earth (Matt 6:19-21). It prioritizes God's kingdom and his righteousness over earthly wealth and personal security (Matt 6:33). The righteousness of true believers is otherworldly.

Beatitudes

Interpretation Question: What are the Beatitudes and why are they important?

The character of the kingdom starts with the Beatitudes in Matthew 5:3-10. The word "beatitude" comes from the Latin word "beatus," which simply means 'bless' or 'bliss'.[4] Each one of the Beatitudes begins with the word "blessed." But the name "beatitude" also is commonly used to describe how each of these attitudes should "be" part of our behavior. They are the "Be Attitudes" that should be in each of our lives.

Each beatitude gives a character trait and then a promise. They are written in a style of writing called an inclusio, where the first and last beatitude end with the same promise—"for the kingdom of heaven belongs to them" (v. 3 and 5).[5] This means that all eight character traits will be in the lives of those who are part of the kingdom of heaven.

This would have been very challenging to the Jews and the religious teachers listening because many believed they were part of the kingdom of heaven simply by virtue of being Jews and because they practiced the external righteousness commanded in the law, as well as the rabbinical traditions in the Talmud. However, those who had truly entered the kingdom would not only have external righteousness but internal righteousness.

As the Beatitudes convicted and challenged Christ's audience then, it should convict and challenge the contemporary church today. Many believe that simply because they prayed a prayer and confessed Jesus as Lord that they are going to heaven. However, if their prayer and confession don't change their lives, then it probably has not changed their eternal destiny.

At the end of the sermon, Christ teaches about this reality. In Matthew 7:22-23, he describes the last days, when many will say to him, "Lord, Lord, we cast out demons and did many mighty works in your name." But he replies, "Depart from me, you workers of iniquity, I never knew you" (paraphrase). These people confessed Christ as Lord and even practiced some good works, but were not saved. They had never been born again. They never experienced a true heart change and, therefore, continued to live a life of iniquity.

Kent Hughes describes this common anomaly in the contemporary church by considering the professed salvation of Mickey Cohen, a flamboyant criminal in the 1950s. The story goes:

> At the height of his career, Cohen was persuaded to attend an evangelistic service at which he showed a surprising interest in Christianity. Hearing of this, and realizing what a great influence a converted Mickey Cohen could have for the Lord, some prominent Christian leaders began visiting him in an effort to convince him to accept Christ. Late one night, after repeatedly being encouraged to open the door of his life on the basis of Revelation 3:20 ("I stand at the door and knock. If anyone hears my voice and opens the door, I will go in and eat with him, and he with me"), Cohen prayed.
>
> Hopes ran high among his believing acquaintances. But with the passing of time no one could detect any change in Cohen's life. Finally they confronted him with the reality that being a Christian meant he would have to give up his friends and his profession. Cohen demurred. His logic? There are "Christian football players, Christian cowboys, Christian politicians; why not a Christian gangster?"[6]

The absurdity of Mickey Cohen's words are repeated in lives of many today. They say, "I'm a Christian, but I can live with my girlfriend out of wedlock." "I'm a Christian but I believe it's OK for me to be in a homosexual relationship." "I believe in Christ, but I like to get drunk, swear like a sailor, and enjoy the things of the world." However, Scripture says that he who is in Christ is a new creation; old things have passed away, and all things become new (2 Cor 5:17). This doesn't mean that there isn't a process of progressive maturity in the life of a true believer. There is. However, if we simply continue living like the world, perhaps, like those in Matthew 7:21-23, we have never been truly born again. From Christ's description of these people, it appears they were in church leadership. Maybe, those who have served as pastors, missionaries, small group leaders, deacons, and worship leaders are more prone to this deception. Like the Pharisees and teachers of the law, they think their intellectual knowledge of Scripture and their external good deeds means that they are truly saved. However, if there is no internal change that leads to continued growth in holiness, they are probably not.

This is why the Beatitudes are so important. They help us discern whether we have truly entered the kingdom of heaven. One day Christ will say to those who have these blessings, "Come, you who are blessed by my Father, inherit the kingdom prepared for you from the foundation of the world" (Matt 25:34). The Beatitudes represent both the nature of kingdom citizens and their aspirations. [7] None of these attitudes are something that we conjure up in our flesh. They are the work of the Holy Spirit in the life of someone who has been born again. And while only Christ modeled these attitudes perfectly, if we do not display them in our lives at all, we may not be part of his kingdom.

In addition, it must be noted that the Beatitudes are not given in a haphazard order. The first four deal primarily with our relationship with God, while the last four deal with our relationship with others. Also, there is a progression in them—each quality leading to another. Poverty of spirit leads to mourning, mourning leads to meekness, and so on. Furthermore, there seems to be a direct connection between the first and fifth (the poor in spirit and being merciful), the second and sixth (mourning and becoming pure in heart), third and seventh (the meek and becoming a peacemaker), and the fourth and eighth (hungering for righteousness and being persecuted for righteousness). In this study, we'll consider the first beatitude: "Blessed are the poor in spirit for the kingdom of heaven belongs to them."

Big Question: What does Christ mean by the first beatitude: "Blessed are the poor in spirit for the kingdom of heaven belongs to them"? What are some practical applications from this beatitude?

The Definition of Blessed

Interpretation Question: What does it mean to be blessed?

1. Blessed means to be happy.

In ancient literature, the word was at times used of people or gods who were unaffected by poverty, disease, misfortune, and death. It reflected an inward contentedness that was not affected by circumstances.[8] In Scripture, it is often used of God, who is the truly happy one. In 1 Timothy 6:15, Paul calls God "the blessed and only Sovereign." Therefore, man can only receive this blessing—this divine happiness—from God, who desires each of his children to have his divine joy. It is seen in Paul, when he said he had learned the secret of being content in all circumstances, whether well-fed or hungry, whether in plenty or in want, because God gave him strength (Phil 4:11-13). The Beatitudes, therefore, mark the attitudes of someone who is truly happy.

Sadly, people often think true happiness comes from possessions, positive circumstances, or relationships. However, true happiness or blessedness is Divine—something only given by God to those living righteously. In addition, the world regularly seeks happiness in sin and the fruits thereof, but true happiness cannot be attained without holiness. There may be a temporary gratification in the pleasures of sin, but ultimately, it brings God's curse and not his blessing.

2. Blessed means to be approved.

Though "blessed" can be translated "happy," it cannot be reduced to only happiness. Happiness ultimately comes as a result of being blessed by God. The word "blessed" also has the sense of being approved. When a man wants to marry a woman, he often asks her father for his blessing—his approval. It's the same here in the Beatitudes. Those who have these characteristics and are growing in them have God's approval—they make God smile. He enjoys them. Therefore, if that is our ultimate desire in life—to please God—then we should listen closely to each of these Beatitudes and pursue them through God's grace, in order to give God pleasure.

3. Blessed means to receive God's favor.

There is also a third sense of the word "Blessed." Not only does God approve of these people and bestow Divine happiness upon them, he also favors them. He lavishly bestows grace, mercy, and peace upon their lives. He favors them in a myriad of ways. Like Psalm 23:6 says, "goodness and faithfulness" follow after them all the days of their lives. Those who personify the Beatitudes are truly blessed by God.

Application Question: What are some ways people pursue happiness apart from God? Why can they never bring lasting happiness or contentment? How do you struggle with pursuing happiness apart from God?

Poverty of Spirit

Interpretation Question: What does it mean to be poor in spirit?

There are two Greek words for "poor"; one refers to the working poor and the other to the truly poor.[9] In Luke 21:2, when Christ described the poor widow, who gave her only two copper coins as an offering, he used the word for the working poor. She was poor with meager resources, but she had something. Then, there was a word used of those who were destitute with no resources and therefore had to beg. In Luke 16:20, it was used of Lazarus who lay at the gate of a rich man's house, longing to eat crumbs that fell from his table. Such beggars often would hold one hand out for money and hide their face with the other hand because of shame. The word "poor" means "to shrink, cower, or cringe," even as beggars did.[10] In fact, a good translation for this word is the "beggarly poor."[11]

When Christ says, "the kingdom of heaven belongs to them," "them" is emphatic in the Greek—literally meaning "them alone."[12] Only these people enter the kingdom of heaven. "Poor in spirit" does not mean that these people think they are worthless for that wouldn't be true; all people are Divine image bearers and therefore have unimaginable worth. Rather, it refers to an awareness and admission of one's utter sinfulness and lack of virtue before God.[13] It is a recognition of one's spiritual bankruptcy.

Interpretation Question: Why is spiritual poverty necessary?

1. Spiritual poverty is necessary for salvation.

This is placed first in the Beatitudes, as it is both the doorway to the kingdom of heaven and also the other attitudes. No one can enter the kingdom of heaven unless they have first come to a place where they recognize their inability to please God and be accepted by him. Hebrews 12:14 says without holiness no one will see God. Because of our sins, we are unacceptable to God and under his wrath (John 3:36). Romans 6:23 says the wages of sin is death. This is where every person who enters the kingdom of heaven begins. They recognize that because of their sin, they are unacceptable to God and under his wrath.

This turns them into the beggarly poor. They cringe before God because they can demand nothing based on their own merit—all they deserve is death. Therefore, they come before God in humility, asking for his grace and mercy. Romans 10:13 says,

"For everyone who calls upon the name of the Lord will be saved." God hears their cry and saves them. Those who have experienced this, and those alone, enter the kingdom of heaven.

In Christ's parable about the Pharisee and the tax collector in Luke 18:9-14, it was the broken tax collector and not the prideful Pharisee who left the temple justified. The Pharisee boasted in his righteous works before God, but the tax collector cried out for God's mercy—he was the broken in spirit. This is the pathway of all true believers. Therefore, poverty of spirit supports the doctrine of justification by faith alone. It affirms that nobody can be saved by baptism, pilgrimage, charity, good works, etc.—only God's grace and mercy can save someone.

This is the opposite of the spirit of the world. Where true believers recognize their spiritual poverty and need for God, the rich in spirit don't. They neither glorify God nor give thanks to him (Rom 1:21). Some even see faith as a crutch—a sign of weakness; it is for people who can't make it in this life on their own. And in one sense, this is true; however, everybody is truly weak, whether they realize it or not. Christ said this to the Church of Laodicea, "Because you say, 'I am rich and have acquired great wealth, and need nothing,' but do not realize that you are wretched, pitiful, poor, blind, and naked" (Rev 3:17). The church considered themselves rich, but they were really poor. In fact, many believe this church was full of unbelievers, as they had not recognized their spiritual poverty and Christ stood outside their hearts knocking—trying to get in (Rev 3:20). Without spiritual poverty—without recognition of our bankruptcy and need for God's salvation—no one will enter the kingdom of heaven.

Have you ever had a time where you recognized your spiritual poverty—that nothing, apart from God's grace, could save you—and cried out for God's grace like a spiritual beggar? If not, you have not entered the kingdom of heaven. It is the poor in spirit, and theirs alone, whose is the kingdom of heaven.

Application Question: Why are so many professing believers self-deceived about their salvation (like the Pharisee, the Church of

Laodicea, and those who approached Christ in Matthew 7:21-23)? How can assurance of salvation be developed?

2. Spiritual poverty is necessary for spiritual growth and being used by God.

Similarly, in Matthew 18:1-4, Christ took a little child in his arms. In the original language, the word "child" is used of an infant or toddler. He says to his disciples, "I tell you the truth, unless you turn around and become like little children, you will never enter the kingdom of heaven!" (v. 3). An infant is utterly helpless; he cries out for the help of his parents for food, covering, and cleaning. This is also true of believers. Romans 8:15 says that we have received the Spirit of adoption by which we cry, "Abba Father." The Spirit of God creates in the hearts of true believers a dependence upon their Daddy. They cry out not only for salvation, but for their daily needs—God's peace, strength, power, and mercy.

After this, Christ also says that those who are like this child are the "greatest in the kingdom of heaven" (v.4). Not only is spiritual poverty the doorway to salvation, it is also the pathway to sanctification. Those who are greatest in the kingdom of heaven—those whom God uses in the greatest manner—are like little children, totally dependent upon their heavenly Father.

The Christian life in many ways is the opposite of the natural life. When a child is born, he is totally dependent upon the parents; however, he quickly begins the process of becoming independent. Where before parents brushed the child's teeth and hair, the child eventually learns how to do this on his own. Progressively, the child grows up and becomes totally independent from his parents. The Christian life is the opposite; when people are born again, they leave their life of independence for a life of spiritual poverty—recognizing their desperate state and need for God's salvation—and crying out for God. But as we mature in Christ, we begin to recognize our spiritual poverty on a deeper level. We start to see how much we need him for every aspect of life. We need him to make it through another day at work. We need his grace for our relationship issues. We need his grace to discern our future. Those maturing in Christ continually learn their dependence upon him.

Often, in order to develop this, God allows trials in our lives. Trials humble us and show us that we are not our own masters. We are not strong enough, smart enough, or wealthy enough. We continue to need God's grace. Through trials, God trains us to call out, "Abba Father!" This is what happened with Paul, as he endured a thorn in his flesh. In 2 Corinthians 12:9, God said to him: "My grace is enough for you, for my power is made perfect in weakness." God allowed weakness in Paul's life to create a greater spiritual poverty, and it was through this spiritual poverty that God's power could be fully displayed.

Therefore, it is the spiritually poor that God uses the most; those who experience this are the greatest in the kingdom of heaven. Martin Luther, who it is often said single-handedly brought the Great Reformation, is famous for this saying, "I have so much to do today that I'm going to need to spend three hours in prayer in order to be able to get it all done."[14] Luther knew his spiritual bankruptcy and thus continually cried out for the riches of God's grace. Those who are poor in spirit are the ones who God uses the most. The kingdom is not just theirs in the future, it is theirs today. The power and authority of the kingdom will abundantly be manifest in their lives.

For example, when God called Moses to lead Israel, Moses gave excuses for why he couldn't speak and lead. When God called Gideon to lead Israel, Gideon declared how he was from the least tribe, and he was least in his family. They were both imperfectly perfect for God, because they recognized their weakness—their spiritual poverty. Therefore, God's power and kingdom could be fully displayed in their lives. Others who might volunteer and declare their credentials and skills are often too strong and too confident for God's purposes. He prefers the weak—the poor in spirit who recognize their poverty. He says to them, "You say you're too weak, but you're perfect for me. My power will be made complete in your weakness." He finds such people and sows his kingdom deep in them so they can help spread his glory throughout the earth.

This was the same spirit displayed in Paul who declared that nothing good dwelled in his flesh (Rom 7:18), that he was chief of sinners (1 Tim 1:15), and least of all God's people (Eph 3:8). Poverty of spirit was also displayed in Christ, who in his incarnation declared, "I tell you the solemn truth, the Son can do nothing on his own initiative, but only what he sees the Father doing" (John 5:19). In John 14:29, he said, "For I have not spoken from my own authority, but the Father himself who sent me has commanded me what I should say and what I should speak." Christ was the epitome of spiritual poverty—he depended totally on the Father, even for what to say. He was just like a child—greatest in the kingdom of heaven. This same spirit must be in us.

Poverty of spirit is the doorway to salvation and the pathway to sanctification. God looks for people with this spirit and uses them greatly for his kingdom (cf. 2 Chr 16:9). With the prideful, he fights against them to make them humble so he may lift them up (James 4:6).

Application Question: How can we tell if we are poor in spirit?

1. If we're poor in spirit, we will be grateful and less likely to complain.

Complainers believe they deserve better—they deserve better food, better housing, better resources, better church services. Their complaints are rooted in pride and an incorrect view of what they truly deserve. However, those who truly recognize their grave condition before the Lord, are thankful even for little things. They thank God for the continual grace and mercy they receive, as they understand that they deserve nothing more than God's wrath. Those who truly know their spiritual poverty are grateful people. They start to learn how to give thanks in all situations for this is God's will for their lives (1 Thess 5:18).

Are you commonly thankful? Or are you prone to complaining?

2. If we're poor in spirit, we will pray often.

Just as physical beggars continually beg for money and food, spiritual beggars continually plead with the Lord for spiritual resources such as grace, strength, peace, and opportunities to serve and bless others. As in 1 Thessalonians 5:17, they begin to learn something of praying without ceasing.

Are you a spiritual beggar? Are you, like Jacob, wrestling with God until he blesses you—meets your needs, empowers you to serve, or changes somebody's life? That's a characteristic of spiritual beggars.

Application Question: How can we grow in awareness of our spiritual poverty?

1. We grow in spiritual poverty by knowing God more.

When we focus on ourselves or others, it creates pride, even if it manifests in insecurity. However, when we focus on God through his Word, prayer, fellowship, and serving, we see our own sin. In Isaiah 6:5, when Isaiah had a vision of God, it led to confessing his sin and that of his people. When Peter recognized Christ, he said, "Go away from me, Lord; I am a sinful man" (Lk 5:8). The more we know God, the more we will see our spiritual poverty and therefore our need for God's mercy and grace.

Are you pursuing a deeper knowledge of God?

2. We grow in spiritual poverty by asking God for it.

Psalm 51:10 says, "Create for me a pure heart, O God! Renew a resolute spirit within me." Like David, we must cry out for a humble spirit that pleases God instead of a prideful spirit that God fights against (James 4:6). Many miss God's best because they have the spirit of this world—pride—instead of the spirit of heaven—a humble, broken spirit.

Are you crying out for more of God's grace?

Application Question: What are some hindrances to spiritual poverty? How is God calling you to pursue growth in spiritual poverty?

Conclusion

When Christ teaches the Beatitudes, he teaches the character traits of those in the kingdom. True believers possess these and yet aspire to grow in them. Have you experienced poverty of spirit? It is the doorway to heaven—for without it, we won't recognize our need for salvation. It is the pathway to spiritual maturity—for those who are like children are greatest in the kingdom. Those who recognize their total dependence upon God can be used greatly by him. Moreover, poverty of spirit is also the stairwell that leads to all the other attitudes. Poverty of spirit leads to mourning, to meekness, to hungering and thirsting for righteousness, and so on. Are you poor in spirit? It is by this characteristic that we will ascend the stairwell of the rest of the Beatitudes. Lord, help us look more like you!

Blessed Are the Mourners

> Blessed are those who mourn, for they will be comforted.
> Matthew 5:4 (NET)

Application Question: In what ways are the characteristics of the kingdom of heaven different from the kingdoms of this earth, especially as seen in the Sermon on the Mount (Matt 5-7)?

The second beatitude declares God's blessing—God's approval and joy—on the lives of those who mourn. It is paradoxical, as are many of the statements in the Beatitudes. Essentially, Christ says, "Happy are the sad." For most, this is the exact opposite of what is logical. Usually, happiness is the avoidance of grief or things that bring pain.

It is important to remember that the Beatitudes are written in a style of writing called an "inclusio." The first and the last beatitude end with the promise, "for the kingdom of heaven belongs to them." This promise fits like two bookends around the Beatitudes, and tells us that each of these characteristics are in those who are part of the kingdom of heaven. The kingdom of heaven is the place of God's rule. It exists not only in heaven, but also on the earth, where people obey and worship him (cf. Matt 6:10). Currently, on the earth, the kingdom exists in spiritual form, as Christ taught that the kingdom of heaven was in our midst (Lk 17:21). One day, it will literally come to the earth at Christ's return. With that said, the kingdom of heaven is the opposite of the kingdom of this world in many ways. While the world says, "Blessed are the strong in spirit—the tough," Christ's kingdom says, "Blessed are the poor in spirit"—those who recognize their weakness before God. While the world says, "Blessed are those who laugh," Christ's kingdom says, "Blessed are those who mourn." In fact, Luke 6:25 says, "'Woe to you who laugh now, for you will mourn and weep." While the world says, "Store up your riches on earth—pursue wealth," Christ's kingdom says, "Store up your riches in heaven" (Matt 6:20 paraphrase). The citizens of the kingdom are different from the people of this world.

These Beatitudes represent the character of the citizens of God's kingdom and, at the same time, their aspirations. Only Christ perfectly models these characteristics, but if they are not in our hearts to the smallest degree, then we might not be part of God's kingdom (cf. Matt 7:21-23).

In this study, we will consider the paradoxical statement, "Blessed are those who mourn, for they will be comforted."

Big Question: What does this beatitude mean and what are its applications for the Christian life?

God Blesses Mourners

Application Question: How can you reconcile Scriptures' commands both to continually rejoice in the Lord and to mourn (Phil 4:4, James 4:8-10, cf. Gal 5:22, Matt 5:4)? How can joy and mourning co-exist?

The New Testament uses nine Greek words for mourning, and Christ uses the strongest of them all.[15] It was used of someone mourning the death of a loved one.[16] It is a present participle, and it means to "continually" mourn. There is a continuous state of mourning in the life of a true believer.

Again, this is paradoxical. Scripture commands the believer to "Rejoice in the Lord" (Phil 4:4) and teaches that joy is a fruit of walking in the Spirit (Gal 5:22). However, there should be a continual mourning alongside the believer's joy that separates him or her from the world.

Interpretation Question: What type of mourning is Christ referring to?

1. It refers to mourning over personal sin.

Obviously, it doesn't refer to mourning over bad circumstances or loss of something precious, since this type of mourning is common to the world as well. It refers to a mourning over personal sin. When people are born again, God changes their relationship to sin. They can't enjoy it, as they once did, or live in it. First John 3:9-10 says,

> Everyone who has been fathered by God does not practice sin, because God's seed resides in him, and thus he is not able to sin, because he has been fathered by God. By this the children of God and the children of the devil are revealed: Everyone who does not practice righteousness—the one who does not love his fellow Christian—is not of God.

When John refers to continuing in sin, he is not saying that Christians don't sin any more. In 1 John 1:8, he said, "If we say we do not bear the guilt of sin, we are deceiving ourselves and the truth is not in us." If we claim to be without sin, the truth—referring to the Gospel—is not in us (cf. 1 John 5:13). We are not truly born again. The Gospel confronts us with our sin and our need for salvation. But when God saves us, he forgives us and changes our relationship to sin. The believer will fall and make mistakes, but the direction of his life is forever changed. He tries to live for God while, at times, stumbling along the way. To "not practice sin" means that the direction of a person's life is still fulfilling his lusts instead of seeking to obey God.

Believers cannot continue in a lifestyle of sin because "God's seed resides" in them; they have been "fathered by God" (1 John 3:9). "God's seed" can be translated "God's nature."[17] At salvation, a believer receives God's nature which exerts a strong influence on a believer toward holiness. It is so radically transforming that a true believer cannot continue in a life of sin. Similarly, in Galatians 5:17, Paul describes how God's Spirit works through our new nature to battle against our flesh—creating a spiritual war in each believer. As a believer walks in the Spirit, he will not fulfill the lusts of the flesh (Gal 5:16). In addition, since being "fathered by God" hinders a believer from continuing in sin, John may also have in mind the reality of God's discipline on his children. Hebrews 12:5-6 and 8 says:

> "My son, do not scorn the Lord's discipline or give up when he corrects you. "For the Lord disciplines the one he loves and chastises every son he accepts."... But if you do not experience discipline, something all sons have shared in, then you are illegitimate and are not sons.

God disciplines his children through the correction of his Word (v. 5); if the believer doesn't respond, God may chasten or spank through storms and trials (v. 6). If the believer continues to persist in sin, God may even take the believer home through an early death. James 5:20 and 1 John 5:16, for example, talk about a sin unto death. We saw this in Acts 5 with Ananias and Sapphira, who lied about their offering and were struck down by the Lord. Also, in 1 Corinthians 11, some believers died as a discipline for abusing the Lord's Supper. Believers cannot go on sinning because they have been born again—God's nature indwells them, and as a child of God, the Lord lovingly disciplines them. God, like any human father, is fully invested in the holiness of his children. He will not let them live in continuous rebellion.

Therefore, at salvation, a true believer's life will change. John says, "By this the children of God and the children of the devil are revealed: Everyone who does not practice righteousness—the one who does not love his fellow Christian—is not of God" (1 John 3:10).

Because of God's nature and his discipline, a true child of God continually mourns over sin. Consider David's experience when he didn't initially repent of sin:

> When I refused to confess my sin, my whole body wasted away, while I groaned in pain all day long. For day and

night you tormented me; you tried to destroy me in the intense heat of summer. (Selah) Then I confessed my sin; I no longer covered up my wrongdoing. I said, "I will confess my rebellious acts to the LORD." And then you forgave my sins. (Selah)
Psalm 32:3-5

When David continued in sin, he was miserable. God's hand was heavy upon him—he was physically sick and maybe even depressed, until he acknowledged his sin and repented. This is true of every believer. Though we may try to live in sin, we can't. For the genuine believer, it will ultimately lead to mourning. Kent Hughes adds: "It is significant that the first of Martin Luther's famous 95 Theses states that the entire life is to be one of continuous repentance and contrition. It was this attitude which caused the apostle Paul to affirm, well along into his Christian life, that he was the chief of sinners (I Timothy 1:15)."[18]

The opposite of mourning is rejoicing or laughter. And this is exactly what we often see in the world. Instead of mourning over sin, they rejoice in it. They laugh about it, as they share stories in the locker rooms. They enjoy it through TV and popular music. They celebrate and promote it, as they parade through the streets. Where the world rejoices, the believer mourns. One of the fruits of true salvation is a mourning over sin. If our profession of Christ has not changed our relationship to sin, then it is likely that our profession has not changed our eternal destiny.

Application Question: In what ways have you experienced personal mourning over sin or even God's discipline?

2. It refers to mourning over the sins of others.

A true believer does not only mourn personal sin, he also mourns the sins of others. A great example of this is Isaiah. When he saw a vision of God's glory in Isaiah 6:5 (NIV), he said, "'Woe to me!' I cried. 'I am ruined! For I am a man of unclean lips, and I live among a people of unclean lips, and my eyes have seen the

King, the LORD Almighty.'" He mourned over his own sin and that of his people. In addition, David said this in Psalm 119:136, "Tears stream down from my eyes, because people do not keep your law." We should mourn over injustice, corruption, sexual immorality, homosexuality, trafficking, the brokenness of families, the sad state of the church, etc. It is this continual mourning that provokes believers to pursue reform.

Sadly, the church often does not mourn, and therefore doesn't seek to be agents of reformation. Instead of mourning over sin, we're either apathetic towards it—where we become spiritually numb, and it doesn't bother us—or worse, we laugh at sin, like the world, and sometimes even enjoy it. We watch it on TV and listen to it on the radio. Satan has a wise strategy. He knows that if he can tempt us to laugh at sin, soon it will lead to acceptance and participation. And that is exactly what has happened to God's people. Consider God's neglected command to Israel to mourn in Isaiah 22:12-13:

> At that time the sovereign master, the LORD who commands armies, called for weeping and mourning, for shaved heads and sackcloth. But look, there is outright celebration! You say, "Kill the ox and slaughter the sheep, eat meat and drink wine. Eat and drink, for tomorrow we die!"

Unfortunately, this is often true of the church—laughing, joking, and celebrating instead of mourning. In James 4:8-10, God also commanded compromising Christians to mourn. James writes,

> Draw near to God and he will draw near to you. Cleanse your hands, you sinners, and make your hearts pure, you double-minded. Grieve, mourn, and weep. Turn your laughter into mourning and your joy into despair. Humble yourselves before the Lord and he will exalt you.

Jesus Christ the Mourner

In the OT, Jeremiah was known as the weeping prophet, as he constantly wept over Israel's sins. In Jeremiah 9:1, he said: "I wish that my head were a well full of water and my eyes were a fountain full of tears! If they were, I could cry day and night for those of my dear people who have been killed." In the NT, Christ is compared to Jeremiah; some actually thought he was a resurrected Jeremiah (Matt 16:14). To that end, Christ is never recorded in the Gospels laughing, though he probably did; however, the narrators do mention his crying twice. He cries over the effects of sin when Lazarus died (John 11:35) and also over the rebellion in Jerusalem (Lk 19:41). Mourning must have been a common character trait of Christ. No doubt, Christ often wept when he saw the false religion of Israel, the selfishness of its leaders, the corruption of the Roman government, and the brokenness in the families. Isaiah prophesied that Christ would be "a man of suffering and familiar with pain" (Is 53:3 NIV). Christ, though full of God's joy, was also a mourner.

In the same way, believers should not only be known by their joy but also by their genuine sorrow. Romans 8:22-23 describes how creation groans, and we groan as well, awaiting our deliverance from sin and full adoption as sons of God.

No doubt, as God commanded Israel through Isaiah and the Jewish Christians through James to mourn (Isaiah 22:12-13, James 4:8-10), he also commands the contemporary church saying, "Groan, weep over your sins and the sins of your community. Mourn over how far your nation has fallen away from God!" Ecclesiastes 3:4 says there is "a time to weep and a time to laugh, a time to mourn and a time to dance." Sadly, the contemporary church has not discerned the seasons. They laugh, when they should weep. They dance, when they should sit in mourning. They binge-watch and listen, when they should close their eyes and ears. Consequently, the church has become largely secular. Many times, it is hard to tell the difference between nonbelievers and Christians. They talk and dress the same, laugh and mourn at the same things, and have the same goals.

God commands us to mourn! Are we mourning? Have we ever grieved over our sin and that of the world, or are we apathetic? Have we lost our sensitivity to sin?

Application Question: Are there any specific ways that God is calling you to mourn personally, locally, or nationally? Are there any ways that God is calling you to be part of efforts toward reform?

God Comforts Mourners

The word "comforted" has the same root as the Greek word "paraclete," which Christ used of the Holy Spirit.[19] In John 14:26, Christ called the Holy Spirit our Helper, Counselor, or Comforter—the one who comes alongside us to help. In 2 Corinthians 1:3-4, God is called, "the Father of mercies and God of all comfort, who comforts us in all our troubles so that we may be able to comfort those experiencing any trouble with the comfort with which we ourselves are comforted by God." In Matthew 5:4, "Blessed are those who mourn for they will be comforted," "they" is emphatic—meaning "they alone." Only those who deeply mourn the effects of sin experience God's comfort.

Interpretation Question: In what ways do mourners experience God's comfort?

1. God comforts mourners through salvation.

When people truly accept the Gospel—that they are sinners under the wrath of God and in need of salvation (John 3:36)—mourning and repentance always follow. John preached repentance (Matt 3:2), Christ preached it (Matt 4:17), and so did his apostles (Acts 2:38). Godly mourning and repentance are necessary for true salvation. In 2 Corinthians 7:10, Paul said, "For sadness as intended by God produces a repentance that leads to salvation, leaving no regret, but worldly sadness brings about death." God comforts mourners with true salvation.

Kent Hughes simply said, "Spiritual mourning is necessary for salvation. No one is truly a Christian who has not mourned over his or her sins. You cannot be forgiven if you are not sorry for your sins."[20]

2. God comforts mourners through forgiving their sins.

Psalm 32:1 says, "How blessed is the one whose rebellious acts are forgiven, whose sin is pardoned!" As with the Beatitudes, "blessed" can be translated, "happy." Divine happiness is bestowed upon believers when God forgives their sins. At the cross, God forgave us judicially. There is now no condemnation for those who are in Christ (Rom 8:1). When God sees us, even though we still fail, he sees the perfect righteousness of his Son (1 Cor 5:21). We are now sons of God. But we still need relational forgiveness to restore intimacy. For example, even though I have a fight with my wife, our legal status doesn't change—she stays my wife. But a fight does affect our intimacy, and therefore, forgiveness is needed. In the same way, with God, we need relational forgiveness on a daily basis. First John 1:9 says, "But if we confess our sins, he is faithful and righteous, forgiving us our sins and cleansing us from all unrighteousness." And when he forgives and cleanses us, we experience his comfort, joy, and intimacy—we experience God's blessing.

3. God comforts mourners by delivering them or others from sin.

God blesses those who mourn, and many times this divine favor is manifest through both being delivered from sin and the fostering of righteousness (cf. Matt 5:6). When God does this in our lives or others, we experience his comfort. Sometimes, he delivers us or a friend from a stronghold; at other times, he revives a church, changes a city or a nation, as we groan and pray over it. Believers experience God's comfort, as he rescues us and others from sin.

4. God comforts mourners through his Word.

Romans 15:4 says, "For everything that was written in former times was written for our instruction, so that through endurance and through encouragement of the scriptures we may have hope." Godly mourning often leads us to Scripture (cf. Ps 119:71), and when it does, God frequently comforts us with its rich truths: He comforts us with the blessed hope of our Lord's return. He comforts us with the hope of our resurrected bodies and that one day we won't struggle with sin or sickness. He comforts us with the hope that he works all things for our good, including our trials and failures. Everything written in Scripture was meant to give us hope. If we are not drinking deeply from Scripture, we will lack much of the comfort and hope God provides.

5. God comforts mourners through the ministry of other believers.

In 2 Timothy 1:16, Paul said, "May the Lord grant mercy to the family of Onesiphorus, because he often refreshed me and was not ashamed of my imprisonment." While Paul was in prison, God refreshed him many times through Onesiphorus. Similarly, as we mourn, God often lavishes his comfort on us through other believers as well.

6. God comforts mourners ultimately at Christ's second coming.

At Christ's return, God will deliver us from the presence of sin altogether. We will have new bodies that are free from pride, lust, anger, and everything that causes stumbling. He will make all things right as he rules on the earth. Revelation 21:4 says, "He will wipe away every tear from their eyes, and death will not exist any more—or mourning, or crying, or pain, for the former things have ceased to exist.'"

Without mourning, we never experience God's comfort. Without mourning sin, no one can be saved. Without mourning, we never break strongholds in our lives. Without mourning, nations aren't changed. The problem with the church is that we don't mourn, and therefore, we often lack God's comfort. God is looking for mourners, so he can bless and use them greatly for his glory. Every great reformer throughout history was a mourner who experienced God's comfort. Nehemiah, for one, fasted and mourned and then God sent him to build the wall around Jerusalem and bring a national revival (cf. Neh 1, 8). In that revival, Nehemiah experienced God's comfort over his mourning.

Are you mourning? Have you experienced God's comfort?

Application Question: In what ways have you experienced God's comfort in the midst of mourning over sin or its effects?

Growth in Spiritual Mourning

Application Question: How can we grow in our spiritual mourning?

1. We grow in spiritual mourning by turning away from sin.

First Thessalonians 5:22 says, "Abstain from every form of evil" (ESV). Sadly, many of us don't do this. Instead of abstaining from sin, we entertain it, talk about it, and soon, lose sensitivity to it. Ultimately, it begins to manifest in our lives. If we are going to be mourners, we must flee from every form of evil. Don't pump it in your ears, don't read about it, don't watch it, and don't joke about it. If we choose to do so, we are on the slow path of decay.

In Psalm 1:1, David said, "Blessed is the man who walks not in the counsel of the wicked, nor stands in the way of sinners, nor sits in the seat of scoffers" (ESV). Many commentators see this as the pathway into depravity. It starts with simply listening to the counsel of the wicked—what sinners are saying. Maybe some rationalize these actions by saying, "We have to know what's going on in the world so we can relate to the lost." Then it leads to standing in the "way"—meaning their behavior has gone from listening to practicing. Then the final stage is sitting with mockers.

This is when believers begin to mock holy things. They say, "Do you really believe that God created the world by his Word? Do you really believe that people should wait to have sex before marriage? Do you really believe homosexuality is sin?" And they mock those who believe such things. But it all starts out with listening to the wrong "counsel." Many have lost the blessing of God simply by what they listened to or read.

If we are going to be blessed mourners, we must stay away from "every form of evil." Exposure to evil slowly hardens our conscience and decays our morals.

2. We grow in spiritual mourning by studying God's Word.

God's Word tells us what is wrong and convicts us of it. It is like a mirror that shows our failures and that of others (James 1:23-25). It is a sharp two-edged sword that pierces our consciences so that we can repent (Heb 4:12). If we don't study God's Word, our consciences will grow calloused and dull.

3. We grow in spiritual mourning by confessing our lack of mourning and praying for God's grace.

We must confess that we have lost sensitivity and are no longer offended at sin, as we should be. We may, in fact, enjoy it and commonly laugh at it. We must pray for grace to be like our Lord who mourned over the world and its sin.

Application Question: Are there any other ways that believers grow in spiritual mourning? How is God calling you to pursue growth in spiritual mourning?

Conclusion

As we conclude, let us consider Ezekiel's vision about Israel's destruction. Ezekiel 9:1-6 says,

Then he shouted in my ears, "Approach, you who are to visit destruction on the city, each with his destructive weapon in his hand!" Next, I noticed six men coming from the direction of the upper gate which faces north, each with his war club in his hand. Among them was a man dressed in linen with a writing kit at his side. They came and stood beside the bronze altar. Then the glory of the God of Israel went up from the cherub where it had rested to the threshold of the temple. He called to the man dressed in linen who had the writing kit at his side. The LORD said to him, "Go through the city of Jerusalem and put a mark on the foreheads of the people who moan and groan over all the abominations practiced in it." While I listened, he said to the others, "Go through the city after him and strike people down; do no let your eye pity nor spare anyone! Old men, young men, young women, little children, and women—wipe them out! But do not touch anyone who has the mark. Begin at my sanctuary!" So they began with the elders who were at the front of the temple.

In the natural world, God sent Babylon to judge Israel, but in the spiritual world, he sent six angels with weapons. In addition, there was one angel with a writing kit, called to mark those who grieved and lamented over all the detestable things done in the city. They mourned over the idolatry, the sexual immorality, and the general dishonoring of God. While others were judged, the mourners were saved. In the same way, there is a group of people on this earth who are part of God's kingdom. They are identified by their mourning over sins—theirs and the world's. And because of this, God marks them; he sets them apart to himself and protects them from his wrath. They will at times be mocked by the world because they are different—because they won't partake in or condone sin. At times, they are even persecuted. However, they are salt and light to the earth. They are a blessing to those who persecute and hate them. And though disliked and, at times, marginalized by the world, God marks them and blesses them. They are members of his kingdom, and one day they will fully inherit it at Christ's coming.

Are you a mourner? Blessed are the mourners for they will be comforted—both in this life and the life to come.

Blessed Are the Meek

> Blessed are the meek, for they will inherit the earth.
> Matthew 5:5 (NET)

Application Question: In what ways is this beatitude paradoxical? How does it differ from the world's philosophy?

The world says it is the proud, the tough, and the aggressive who inherit the earth. It is the survival of the fittest. But Christ says the meek will inherit the land. It is a paradoxical statement, just as the other Beatitudes are.

As we consider this—it is important to remember that the Beatitudes are characteristics of those who enter the kingdom of heaven. The Beatitudes begin and end with "for the kingdom of heaven belongs to them." If these characteristics are not in our lives, however imperfectly, we are not part of the kingdom of heaven.

Again, there is a progression within these characteristics. It starts with being poor in spirit. This means that people intellectually recognize that there is nothing in them that would commend them to God. They are like beggars with no spiritual credit to their account. It is the poor in spirit, and them alone, who are part of the kingdom of heaven. When people recognize their sin and therefore poverty before God, this leads to an emotional response—mourning over sin. From these two attitudes arises the third beatitude, "meekness." Those who recognize their sin and mourn over it become the meek who inherit the earth.

In this study, we will consider meekness and the promise to the meek.

Big Question: What does it mean to be meek and receive the earth? Also, what applications can we take from this beatitude?

Meekness

Interpretation Question: What does it mean to be meek and what does it look like practically?

First, it should be said that there is no one English word that can fully capture the meaning of the Greek word. "Prautes" was used of a soothing medicine, a soft breeze, and a trained animal.[21] It is typically translated meek, humble, or gentle. Since none of these fully capture the meaning, we'll consider what it looks like to be meek.

1. The meek are self-controlled or Divinely controlled.[22]

As mentioned, the Greek word was used of a formerly wild animal that had been broken and trained by its master. Previously, the animal could not be ridden or controlled, but after being trained, it followed the master's instruction. This is true of believers; when we first come to Christ, we often are wild and don't fully submit to or trust our Master. However, through both trials and blessings, God teaches us to fully trust and obey him.

We saw this in the life of Abraham. When he first began to follow the Lord, he left his home and family to go to the land to which God called him. However, Genesis 11 tells us that he didn't leave his entire family behind and that he stopped before reaching Canaan. He brought his father and nephew and tarried in Haran for many years until his father died. Abraham didn't fully obey God—his obedience was delayed and partial. Then when he finally got to the promised land, there was a famine. Therefore, he immediately left and went to Egypt where he suffered by briefly losing his wife to Pharaoh (Gen 12). Later, as Abraham awaited the promised child, he took things into his own hands by marrying his wife's servant, Hagar (Gen 16). This caused great strife in his family—strife which continues today between Jews and Arabs.

However, in Genesis 22, when God calls him to sacrifice his son, Isaac, he immediately obeys though it would have cost him greatly. Hebrews 11:19 says he was willing to sacrifice his son because he believed God would raise him from the dead. Through his years of walking with God, and at times stumbling, he learned to continually trust and submit to God—he grew in meekness. Instead of responding with delayed obedience or clear disobedience, when God made him wait, put him in a trial, or commanded something perplexing, he learned to immediately obey. Abraham grew in meekness—he was God-controlled.

Young Christians often get mad at God when things don't go their way. They are like partially trained horses that don't fully trust their Master and occasionally try to buck him off. Psalm 32:8-9 says:

> I will instruct and teach you about how you should live. I will advise you as I look you in the eye. Do not be like an unintelligent horse or mule, which will not obey you unless they are controlled by a bridle and bit.

As immature believers, God must, at times, exert force on us to obey. He must train us to be meek. But as we mature, his Word and pleasure become sufficient.

Application Question: In what ways have you experienced this gradual growth in submission to God and his Word, even as Abraham did?

2. The meek are gentle in response to personal offense, as they trust God with judgment.

Christ taught this in various ways and demonstrated it with his life. In Matthew 5:38-41, he teaches that if someone slaps us on the cheek, we should turn the other cheek. And, if someone makes us go one mile, we should willingly go two miles. If someone wants our shirt, we should give our jacket as well. This is the type of person that the world would call "weak," but it is not weakness—it is power under control. It is not that the person cannot fight back, it's that he won't fight back. He trusts God to fight his battles; it is his job to bless.

We saw this in Joseph's response to his brothers who had previously sold him into slavery. After Joseph's father died, the brothers threw themselves down before Joseph—declaring that they were his slaves and pleading with him to not punish them. In Genesis 50:19-21, he responds:

> "Don't be afraid. Am I in the place of God? As for you, you meant to harm me, but God intended it for a good purpose, so he could preserve the lives of many people, as you can see this day. So now, don't be afraid. I will provide for you and your little children." Then he consoled them and spoke kindly to them.

When he says, "Am I in the place of God?", this means that it was not Joseph's right to judge them. It was God's. Joseph chose to bless them and provide for their children. Paul taught the same thing in Romans 12:19-21:

> Do not avenge yourselves, dear friends, but give place to God's wrath, for it is written, "Vengeance is mine, I will repay," says the Lord. Rather, if your enemy is hungry, feed him; if he is thirsty, give him a drink; for in doing this you will be heaping burning coals on his head. Do not be overcome by evil, but overcome evil with good.

Obviously, this is perfectly modeled in Christ. Peter said this about him, "When he was maligned, he did not answer back; when he suffered, he threatened no retaliation, but committed himself to God who judges justly" (1 Pet 2:23).

How do you respond when people hurt or insult you? The meek respond with gentleness. They bless and don't curse. They seek to serve, instead of seeking revenge, as they entrust judgment to God.

Application Question: Why is it so difficult to leave justice with God in regards to personal offense? Should we, at times, defend ourselves? If so, when?

3. The meek are righteously angry at injustice towards others and dishonor toward God.

Righteous anger is a great virtue. Psalm 7:11 describes how God is angry at sin all day long; therefore, we should be as well. Without righteous anger, sin continues, people are abused, God is blasphemed, and nothing ever changes. Often, sin continues simply because we are not angry enough. We are apathetic and unconcerned about the rampant sin of society, the pain of others, and the injustices happening throughout the world; therefore, evil continues to spread.

The meek respond gently to personal offense but with righteous anger when others are injured or treated unjustly. Again, we see this perfectly modeled in Christ. When he was personally insulted, he was like a lamb. He never retaliated and often said nothing. He was powerful; he could have called myriads of angels to defend him, but he didn't. He willingly submitted himself to God's perfect will—including death for our sins. However, when it came to others being mistreated or God being dishonored, he was like a lion. He called the Pharisees serpents and whitewashed tombs. He went into the temple twice with a whip and drove out those cheating others and dishonoring God.

In Numbers 12, Moses was called the meekest man on the earth (v. 3). When his sister and brother were angry with him for marrying an Ethiopian woman, he did and said nothing. God defended him by judging his sister and making her leprous. In response, Moses pleaded for mercy and God healed her. But when Israel sinned against God by worshipping the golden calf, he broke the stone tablets, which the Ten Commandments were written on, ground up the idol and made the Israelites drink it (Ex 32). He was righteously angry, but not selfishly angry.

William Barclay translated the word "meek" as "Blessed are those who are always angry at the right time, and never angry at the wrong time."[23] Furthermore, he added:

> If we ask what the right time and the wrong time are, we may say as a general rule for life that it is never right to be angry for any insult or injury done to ourselves—that is something that no Christian must ever resent—but that it is often right to be angry at injuries done to other people. Selfish anger is always a sin; selfless anger can be one of the great moral dynamics of the world.[24]

Application Question: In what ways have you experienced righteous anger when others were hurt or God was dishonored? How did you handle it?

4. The meek are humble before God and others.

They are humble because they know their spiritual poverty—how they fall short of God's glory—and continually mourn it. Where the prideful desire to exalt themselves and, in the process, often put others down, the humble desire for God to be exalted and for others to be lifted up. Philippians 2:3-4 says, "Instead of being motivated by selfish ambition or vanity, each of you should, in humility, be moved to treat one another as more important than yourself. Each of you should be concerned not only about your own interests, but about the interests of others as well." This is what Christ did, as he became a man and offered his life for others (Phil 2:5-11). This is how Paul was when he said that he would rather be cursed and cut off from Christ so that Israel may be saved (Rom 9:2-3). The humble seek the interests of God and others over their own. Are you humble?

Application Question: How would you describe the difference between pride and humility? How should humility be practiced?

Tests of Meekness

Application Question: How can we tell if we are meek?

We can discern if we are meek by honestly answering a few simple questions:

1. Do I submit to God and his Word? Or do I get angry at God and rebel against him, especially when times are hard?

2. How do I respond when people accuse or hurt me? In general, do I let God defend me or do I fight for my rights? Martin Lloyd Jones said it this way: "The test of meekness is not whether we can say we are poor sinners, but what we do when others call us vile sinners" (paraphrase).[25]

3. Am I righteously angry when people dishonor God and hurt others? Or am I apathetic when it comes to the honor of God and the pain of others?

4. Am I humble or prideful? Am I pursuing the benefit and blessing of others above my own? Or is my prosperity the driving force in my life? Is it important for others to think highly about me? Or am I content with God's pleasure and approval?

Application Question: Which characteristic of the meek stood out most to you and why? Which aspect do you feel most challenged to grow in? What other questions are good tests of our meekness?

The Necessity of Meekness

Application Question: Why is it necessary to be meek?

1. Meekness provides a proof of salvation.

Again, when Christ said, "they will inherit the earth," "they" is emphatic—meaning "they alone." When people have truly been born again, they recognize their spiritual poverty and are led to mourn. This creates meekness in their lives. Because they see their sin before God, it creates a humility—leading them to submit to Christ's lordship. They begin to imperfectly control their anger. Instead of seeking revenge, they begin to bless their enemies, instead of cursing them.

Christ says if these characteristics are not showing up in our lives, we are not part of his kingdom. The world is wild and unruly—they don't obey God. But the believer has submitted control of his life to God and wants to obey him. Since he has been forgiven so much, he forgives others when they fail him. Because God's nature abides in him, he is angry at his sin and that of others, so he fights against it.

Is meekness being demonstrated in your life—bringing assurance of salvation? Kent Hughes describes the importance of meekness for assurance this way:

> Again, this is not to suggest that you are not a Christian if you fall into these sins [referring to being harsh, grasping, vengeful, and uncontrollable], but rather to point out that if they are part of your persona, if you are a self-satisfied "Christian" who thinks that the lack of gentleness and meekness is "just you" and people will have to get used to it, if you are not repentant, you are probably not a Christian.
>
> Jesus' words are not demanding perfection. The point is, however, that if a gentle/meek spirit is not at least imperfectly present in your life, if it is not incipient and growing, you may very well not have the smile of Christ, which is everything.[26]

2. Meekness is necessary as an act of obedience.

In Scripture, God commands believers to be meek. Colossians 3:12 says, "Put on then, as God's chosen ones, holy and beloved, compassionate hearts, kindness, humility, meekness, and patience" (ESV). Many times, we must respond in meekness simply as an act of obedience to our heavenly Father.

3. Meekness is necessary to receive and understand God's Word.

In the ESV, James 1:21 says, "Therefore put away all filthiness and rampant wickedness and receive with meekness the implanted word, which is able to save your souls." In order to receive the seed of the Word of God, we must have meek hearts—hearts willing to submit to our Master. If we rebel and fight against what Scripture teaches, the Word of God will never take root in our lives to save or sanctify us.

In fact, we need meekness—a willingness to submit to our Master's Words—to even understand Scripture. John 7:17 says, "If anyone wants to do God's will, he will know about my teaching, whether it is from God or whether I speak from my own authority." If we don't want to do God's will, we won't be able to truly understand God's Word. We'll twist and pervert Scripture to make it fit our desires, or we'll reject it outright. We need this meek spirit in order to receive and understand Scripture.

4. Meekness is necessary in order to properly teach Scripture.

In 1 Peter 3:15 (NIV), Peter said:

But in your hearts revere Christ as Lord. Always be prepared to give an answer to everyone who asks you to give the reason for the hope that you have. But do this with gentleness and respect

"Gentleness" is the same word for "meekness." Without gentleness, we'll harm people with God's Word. We'll argue, fight, and push people away. Paul said in Ephesians 4:15 that we must speak the truth in love. Without humility, we'll puff ourselves up with our knowledge and condemn others. We'll be like the Pharisees who sought to hurt and control others with Scripture, instead of edifying and healing them. In addition, without righteous anger—an important aspect of meekness—people will never recognize the seriousness of sin. We need meekness to properly teach God's Word.

Application Question: What are your thoughts about the importance of meekness for assurance of salvation and to receive, understand, and teach Scripture? What are some other reasons why meekness is necessary?

Growth in Meekness

Application Question: How can we grow in meekness?

We develop meekness through several ways:

1. To grow in meekness, we must ask God for it.

Meekness is a supernatural characteristic. It is a fruit of the Holy Spirit (Gal 5:23). Pride, lack of self-control, and fits of rage are fruits of our flesh (Gal 5:19-20). We must cry out for the Holy Spirit to bear the fruits of humility, self-control, and gentleness in our lives.

2. To grow in meekness, we must yoke ourselves to Christ, in discipleship.

Christ said this in Matthew 11:29, "Take my yoke on you and learn from me, because I am gentle and humble in heart, and you will find rest for your souls." Again, "gentle" can be translated "meek." In biblical times, a young ox was yoked to an experienced ox so that he could be trained. Christ is the perfectly meek one. As we commit to Christ and abide in him through praying, studying his Word, serving, etc., he will train us to be like him. He will train us to keep our mouths closed when people criticize or hurt us and to trust that God will defend us. He'll teach us to be righteously angry—consumed with God's glory and justice for all.

Are you allowing yourself to be trained by Christ—the one who submitted his rights to God and trusted God's judgment? Or are you allowing yourself to be trained by the world—seeking the earth now instead of in eternity?

3. To grow in meekness, we must grow in faith.

In the same way, a wild horse must learn to trust the master in order to be tamed, we must also learn to trust God to grow in meekness. This concept is also reflected in Psalm 37, in which Matthew 5:5 was originally quoted. David, the author of this wisdom Psalm, begins it with:

> Do not fret when wicked men seem to succeed! Do not envy evildoers! For they will quickly dry up like grass, and wither away like plants. Trust in the LORD and do what is right! Settle in the land and maintain your integrity!
> Psalm 37:1-3

It is easy to focus on the prosperity of the world who do not acknowledge God and sometimes persecutes the just. This often leads to discouragement and, at times, even following the world's path. In Psalm 37:10-11, David said: "Evil men will soon disappear; you will stare at the spot where they once were, but they will be gone. But the oppressed will possess the land and enjoy great prosperity."

Similarly, in Psalm 73, another wisdom Psalm, Asaph said his feet almost slipped, as he envied the arrogant and their prosperity (Ps 73:2-3). It wasn't until he went into God's sanctuary that he understood their ultimate end and found strength to persevere (Ps 73:17).

Likewise, if we are to inherit the land and God's blessings, we must go into God's sanctuary and see the end of the wicked—those who live for this world. We must learn to trust God to defend and reward us, and ultimately to judge the ungodly.

How do we grow in faith—our trust in God?

In short, Romans 10:10 says faith comes by hearing and hearing by the Word of God. As we live in God's Word, our minds become transformed by it. We begin to understand that in God's economy, the first will be last and the last will be first. It is the meek and humble, not the proud and arrogant, who inherit the land. Without living in God's Word, our faith will be weak, and we'll get discouraged and possibly start following the path of the world—seeking to inherit the earth now.

Application Question: How is God calling you to pursue growth in meekness?

Inherit the Earth

Interpretation Question: What does it mean to inherit the earth?

To inherit the earth seems to have three aspects:

1. In the future, the meek will inherit the earth at Christ's coming.

    When God created the earth, he gave dominion of it to man. However, when Adam sinned, paradise was lost. Satan became the prince of this world, and sin brought this world into bondage. Instead of staying in a state of newness and fruitfulness, it decays, grows thorns, and causes pain. However, one day, at Christ's return, he will give the world again to the meek. At that time, there will be a renewal of the earth—the lion will lie down with the lamb, the cow will feed with the bear, and children will lead them (Isaiah 11). There will be perfect peace in the world. Paradise will be ruled by the meek, as they are co-heirs with Christ (Rom 8:17).

2. Presently, the meek inherit the earth in the sense that they are not owned by their possessions.

Kent Hughes said it this way:

> But there is also a present inheritance that abundantly enriches our earthly existence. There is a sense in which those who set their minds on riches never possess anything. This was given classic expression by one of the world's wealthiest men when asked how much is enough money. "Just a little bit more," he answered. He owned everything, yet possessed nothing!
>
> It is the meek who own the earth now, for when their life is free from the tyranny of "just a little more," when a gentle spirit caresses their approach to their rights, then they possess all.[27]

The world is constantly ruled by the spirit of more. They need the newest phone, the newest laptop, the newest clothes, and the newest car, and therefore never really possess anything. Instead, things possess them. However, when believers don't focus on the things of this world, it allows them to "seek first the kingdom of heaven" and Christ says, "all these things will be added unto them" (Matt 6:33 paraphrase). God meets their needs now, and one day, they will possess all things.

3. Presently, the meek inherit the earth in that God often exalts them to places of leadership and authority now.

God opposes the proud but gives grace to the humble (James 4:6). He took Moses who was the meekest man on the earth and put him in leadership over his chosen people. He took Joseph from slavery and prison and made him second in command over Egypt. He took David, a shepherd boy, and made him king over Israel. God blesses the meek and often gives them the land—leadership and authority—now.

"Blessed are the meek, for they [alone] will inherit the earth." Only these people will receive the eternal inheritance of the earth. And only these people possess the earth now. For most, the world and its things possess them. God often places the meek in places of authority and leadership now, which is just a foretaste of eternity.

Application Question: What do you think about the statement, "Most people don't possess things; things possess them"? In what ways is this true? Why should believers relate differently to earthly possessions? How have you seen or experienced God putting the meek in places of authority now?

Conclusion

The world says it is the proud, the tough, and the aggressive who inherit the earth. It is the survival of the fittest. But Christ says it is the meek—the ones who submit to God and trust him to defend them. It is those who humble themselves before their Master and submit to his leading who inherit the land.

Are you one of the meek? It is the meek, and the meek alone, who inherit the land. Thank you, Lord. Amen!

Blessed Are the Hungry

> Blessed are those who hunger and thirst for righteousness, for they will be satisfied.
> Matthew 5:6 (NET)

One of the greatest indicators of health is hunger. When a person isn't feeling well and he visits the doctor, the doctor often asks, "Have you been eating?" In the same way that physical hunger helps us discern our physical health, spiritual hunger helps us discern our spiritual health. It even displays if we are spiritually alive at all.

It is good to remember that the Beatitudes encompass both the character and aspirations of citizens of the kingdom of heaven. The first and last beatitudes end with the promise, "for the kingdom of heaven belongs to them." This style of writing tells us that each of these characteristics will be present in the life of somebody who has entered the kingdom—somebody who is born again. But not only do these characteristics tell us if we are born again—spiritually alive—they tell us if we are spiritually healthy. No one has ever perfectly modeled these characteristics except for Christ, but if Christ lives in us, they will be displayed in our lives to some extent. Because they are the characteristics of our Lord, we should continually aspire to grow in them.

In this study, we will consider the fourth beatitude, "Blessed are those who hunger and thirst for righteousness, for they will be satisfied."

Big Question: What does it mean to hunger and thirst for righteousness and thus be filled? How should this beatitude be applied?

Hunger and Thirst for Righteousness

Interpretation Question: What type of hunger and thirst is Christ referring to?

The words for "hunger" and "thirst" are not words used of somebody who is casually hungry and thirsty. They refer to someone who is starving for food and someone who will die without a drink.[28] This is something most people from developed countries know nothing about. When we're hungry, we open the refrigerator and grab a snack. If we're thirsty, we pour a cup of water. But the ancient world, to whom Christ spoke, knew hunger and thirst well. Most families in Palestine could only eat meat once a week. Wages were low, if they existed at all, and did not allow for luxuries—it was just enough to survive. Travel often led people through large deserts with no water; therefore, thirst was a common companion.[29] When a person is desperately hungry and thirsty, nothing else will satisfy them—not a beautiful sunrise or sunset, not entertainment or rest—only food and water will do.

The Greek words for "hunger" and "thirst" are present participles meaning a continual hungering and thirsting.[30] There is a continual hunger and thirst in the life of true believers that separates them from the world. What is that hunger and thirst for? According to Christ, it is for righteousness.

There is something unusual in this Greek statement. Typically, Greek verbs like "hunger" and "thirst" have partial objects. For example, "I am hungry for some bread" or "I'm thirsty for some water." But Christ uses an unqualified object. It's like saying, "I'm hungry for all the bread" or "all the water." True believers are hungry for complete righteousness—not partial righteousness.[31] It's not OK to love God, and yet compromise in their language, practice dishonesty, or commit immorality. These people want to be fully righteous—partial righteousness won't do. They want to be perfect like their Lord. God created us for this. Ephesians 2:10 says, "For we are his workmanship, having been created in Christ Jesus for good works that God prepared beforehand so we may do them."

Application Question: What types of righteousness or good works do true believers hunger and thirst for?

1. Believers hunger and thirst for Christ's imputed righteousness.

God, initially, creates this hunger in an unbeliever as he is convicted of his sin and failures before God. Romans 3:23 says, "for all have sinned and fall short of the glory of God." Romans 6:23 says, "For the payoff of sin is death". God made man in the image of God—to be holy. However, all men have failed to be like God in action, word, and thought. Therefore, because God is righteous and holy, we are under his wrath and deserving of death (cf. John 3:36). Hebrews 12:14 (NIV) says "without holiness no one will see God."

Therefore, how can man have a right relationship with God? How can a person be saved and have eternal life—abiding with God forever? Two thousand years ago, Christ, the Son of God, came to the earth as a man and lived the perfect life that we could never live. He always did what the Father told him to do. He always said what the Father said. He was the perfect child. However, the world, who loves sin and therefore hates righteousness, rejected and crucified Christ. On the cross, Christ not only suffered the scorn of man, but the wrath of God. Christ took the wrath we deserved for our sin so he could offer those who come to him the gift of perfect righteousness.

Romans 3:21-22 says,

> But now apart from the law the righteousness of God (which is attested by the law and the prophets) has been disclosed—namely, the righteousness of God through the faithfulness of Jesus Christ for all who believe. For there is no distinction

To all who believe in Christ—acknowledging in his life, death, and resurrection for the sins of the world—and turn from their sin to follow him, he imparts his perfect righteousness to their account. Second Corinthians 5:21 says, "God made the one who did not know sin to be sin for us, so that in him we would become the righteousness of God."

Those who are truly born again have gone through the steps of the Beatitudes: They recognize their spiritual poverty, as they have fallen short of God's glory—even their righteous deeds are as filthy rags before God (Is 64:6). They mourned because of their sin and because they were under God's judgment. They became the meek who submitted to the Lordship of Christ and began to hunger and thirst for righteousness. Therefore, God saved them by imparting the perfect righteousness of Jesus to their account. They are now sons and daughters of God and will dwell eternally with him.

Have you recognized your sinfulness and inability before God? No amount of work will save you: church attendance won't, taking the Lord's Supper won't, and neither will baptism. Our only hope for salvation is Christ's perfect work on our behalf.

While believers hunger and thirst to be made right before God, the world is content—they say, "I'm a pretty good person; I believe God will accept me into heaven," or they have no desire to be right with God at all. Others desire to be right with God, but instead of recognizing their inability to save themselves, they try to earn their salvation through works. Our only hope for salvation is Christ's perfect work and sacrifice for our sins. When God resurrected Christ, he was saying, "I accept my Son's sacrifice on your behalf." Romans 4:25 says, "He was given over because of our transgressions and was raised for the sake of our justification."

Have you experienced Christ's imputed righteousness? Romans 10:13 tells us that anyone who calls upon the name of the Lord shall be saved. We must turn from our sin and accept Christ as our Lord and Savior, and he will save us.

2. Believers hunger and thirst for practical righteousness.

Those who have been made righteous by Christ in salvation will naturally hunger and thirst to serve God and others through righteous works. Righteous deeds are not the root of salvation, as taught by all other religions; they are the fruit of true salvation—of already being made righteous before God. James said that faith without accompanying works is dead (James 2:17). If our profession of faith does not produce a lifestyle of hungering for and practicing good works, our profession is false. In Matthew 7:21, Christ said, "Not everyone who says to me, 'Lord, Lord,' will enter the kingdom of heaven—only the one who does the will of my Father in heaven." Only those who do the will of the Father will enter heaven. Serving and obeying God is a proof of true salvation. This hunger for righteousness begins when we are spiritually born at salvation, just as hunger for food happens immediately with natural birth. A healthy baby desires the nutrients that come from his or her mother. And it's the same for a spiritual baby—he will hunger and thirst for righteousness and God will fill him. God fills believers throughout this life with righteous works and deeds, and one day, he will ultimately fill them, as they become perfect like Christ (cf. 1 John 3:2). They will serve Christ and others eternally in the coming kingdom (cf. Lk 19:17,19).

Application Question: What are some specific aspects of practical righteousness that believers hunger and thirst for?

- A practical righteousness that believers hunger and thirst for is the salvation of souls.

In John 4, we see the story of Christ meeting with the woman at the well. After talking with her briefly, she leaves to gather her Samaritan friends so they can meet the Messiah. The disciples approach Christ about getting some food to eat. However, Christ sharply responds to them saying: "My food is to do the will of him who sent me and to finish his work. Lift up your eyes, the fields are ripe for harvest!" (John 4:32-35, paraphrase). Soon after, many Samaritans came to hear him speak and believed in him (39-40).

It is the most natural thing for new believers to want to share their faith with all who will listen. They share it with their friends, family, co-workers, and even strangers. Often, they are viewed as over-zealous. But such enthusiasm is simply the natural hunger of someone who has been born again—they want others to know Christ.

It is good for us to remember that hunger is a sign of our spiritual health. Are you still hungry for souls to know Christ?

- A practical righteousness that believers hunger and thirst for is knowing God's Word.

When Christ was tempted in the wilderness by Satan to turn a rock into bread, Christ responded, "Man does not live by bread alone, but by every word that comes from the mouth of God" (Matt 4:4). No doubt, while Christ fasted for forty days, he was eating and drinking God's Word. In fact, his very response came from Deuteronomy 8:3, and every other time he was tempted, he responded with Scripture.

It is the most natural thing for believers to desire God's Word when they have truly been born again. Before salvation, they are apathetic towards Scripture. They don't typically desire to read it, study it, listen to it being taught, or obey it. But when they are born again, it becomes their food. Like Job, they cry out, "I love your words even more than my daily bread" (Job 23:12, paraphrase). Like David, they declare, "O how I love your law! All day long I meditate on it" (Ps 119:97). Furthermore, he cries, "Seven times a day I praise you because of your just regulations" (Ps 119: 164).

Are you still delighting in God's Word and meditating on it all day long? Or has it become a chore and a burden?

- A practical righteousness that believers hunger and thirst for is the knowledge of God.

The Psalmist says:

> O God, you are my God! I long for you! My soul thirsts for you, my flesh yearns for you, in a dry and parched land where there is no water.
> Psalm 63:1

> As a deer longs for streams of water, so I long for you, O God! I thirst for God, for the living God. I say, "When will I be able to go and appear in God's presence?"
> Psalm 42:1

Moses who spoke to God face to face and had a more intimate relationship with God than other prophets, cried out, "Show me your glory!" (Ex 33:18). Paul, who met Christ in a vision at his salvation, who received the Gospel by a revelation of Christ (Gal 1:12), who went to the third heaven and heard unexplainable words (2 Cor 12:4), said that he counted everything a loss to gain Christ and that he desired to know him more intimately by experiencing the power of the resurrection, fellowshipping with his sufferings, dying like Christ, and resurrecting like him (Phil 3:8-10).

Though a believer meets Christ at salvation, that only whets his appetite. There should be a continual hungering to know and experience God more.

Are you still hungering and thirsting to know God and experience him?

- A practical righteousness that believers hunger and thirst for are the specific works God has called them to.

Each believer is God's workmanship; he has fashioned every believer in a specific way to serve him (Eph 2:10). As we walk with God, he cultivates both our desire and aptitude for these specific works, and then gives us opportunities to serve. Philippians 2:13 (NIV) says he works in us to "will" and to "act" according to his good pleasure. For some that will include parenting and raising godly children; for others that will include serving in business, education, or politics; for others, it might include serving in full-time ministry. As we walk with God, he cultivates a hunger and thirst for the specific righteous deeds he has called us to, which will glorify his name.

Application Question: How would you rate your hunger from 1 to 10 for the various practical righteous works mentioned—knowing God, his Word, and evangelizing? What specific and unique works has God cultivated a desire for in your life? How are you serving or pursuing service in that unique capacity?

Lack of a Spiritual Appetite

Application Question: Why do believers often lack a spiritual appetite?

There could be many reasons for lack of a spiritual appetite:

1. Some lack a spiritual appetite simply because they have never been born again.

    A spiritual appetite is a necessary proof of salvation. Jonathan Edwards called these "religious affections." We may have seasons when we are not as hungry, but if we have never experienced these affections, then we have never been born again. A continuous lack of appetite might represent a lack of true life.

2. Some lack a spiritual appetite simply because their diet is unhealthy.

    Parents often tell their children: "Don't eat sweets before dinner because they will ruin your appetite!" In the same way, many Christians are feasting on sin and things of the world, and these rob them of their spiritual appetite and therefore the blessing of God. God approves and smiles upon those who are desperately hungry for righteousness.

We see another good picture of this in 1 Peter 2:1-2. Peter says, "So get rid of all evil and all deceit and hypocrisy and envy and all slander. And yearn like newborn infants for pure, spiritual milk, so that by it you may grow up to salvation."

He calls for the believers to get rid of various types of sin, and then calls them to yearn for spiritual milk—referring to the Word—like newborn babies so that they can grow. The implication is that feasting on sin and the things of the world hinders our appetite for the things of God. John said it this way: "Do not love the world or the things in the world. If anyone loves the world, the love of the Father is not in him" (1 John 2:15). Essentially, he states, "You can't love both." If we are loving the things of this world—things that dishonor God or don't acknowledge him—we will find our love for God decreasing. In the same way, when we are constantly feasting on things that acknowledge and honor God, our love for the things of the world will decrease and our love for God will increase.

3. Some lack a spiritual appetite simply because of busyness.

When it comes to natural hunger, many neglect eating simply because they are too busy. In the midst of their busyness, they don't notice or pay attention to their hunger and therefore skip meals. No doubt, this happens spiritually, as well.

Certainly, we get a picture of this in the story of Mary and Martha in Luke 10. Christ visited the two sisters' house. While there, Martha was busy being a good host—serving everybody. The problem, as she saw it, was that her sister, Mary, was simply sitting at Jesus' feet while he taught. Martha became angry and confronted Jesus. She said to him, "Tell my sister to help me." Christ simply responded, "Martha, Martha, you are busy about many things. She has chosen what is better, and it will not be taken from her" (38-42, paraphrase).

What's paradoxical is that Martha was doing a good thing; she was serving God and others. However, *good* things are most commonly the enemy of the *best* things. Many are just like this.

They are busy doing good things like work, ministry, recreation, etc.; however, they are neglecting what's most important. They don't have time to pray, study God's Word, or worship; therefore, their spiritual appetite for these things decreases.

Personally, I have noticed that when I'm implementing the spiritual discipline of Sabbath—where I take one day a week to cease working and rest—that it rejuvenates me not only physically but spiritually. I find that I'm more thankful and joyful. I desire to pray, read God's Word, and serve more. However, when I neglect my Sabbath, I start going into survival mode. I'm not thankful, joyful, or prayerful—I'm just trying to survive.

Are you still spiritually hungry? If not, why not?

Application Question: What practices, or neglect of practices, often leads to a lack of spiritual appetite in your life?

Fostering a Healthy Appetite

Application Question: How can we develop a healthy appetite for the things of God?

1. To foster a healthy appetite, we must confirm that we are born again.

We cannot conjure up a desire for the things of God. Romans 8:7 says, "because the outlook of the flesh is hostile to God, for it does not submit to the law of God, nor is it able to do so." First Corinthians 2:14 tells us,

> The unbeliever does not receive the things of the Spirit of God, for they are foolishness to him. And he cannot understand them, because they are spiritually discerned.

An appetite for the things of God is a supernatural work that God does within a person in order for him to respond to God in salvation (cf. Eph 2:8-9) and obey him (Phil 2:13). Therefore, if one has never accepted Christ or if one suspects that his profession is not genuine, he should confess his sins before God and commit to following Christ as Lord and Savior (cf. Rom 10:9-10, 13). God will save him, fill him with the Holy Spirit, and give him a new nature, which desires the things of God.

2. To foster a healthy appetite, we must stay away from appetite-killers.

We must repent of any sins—turning away from ungodly entertainment, relationships, and other practices. With good things, we must be disciplined with them or let them go as well. We must be vigilant in protecting our spiritual appetite.

3. To foster a healthy appetite, we must eat.

If a natural baby doesn't eat for a day, the parents will take him to the doctor and that doctor will connect the baby's arm to an IV. The doctor will force-feed the child because if the child doesn't eat, he'll die. We should do the same spiritually. Often the wisest thing we can do when we lack a spiritual appetite is force-feed ourselves. We should wake up in the morning and get into the Word and prayer. Before bed, we should do likewise. We should take advantage of spiritual opportunities like small groups, worship services, and other ministries. We must force-feed ourselves in order to cultivate our hunger.

4. To foster a healthy appetite, we must eat with others.

One of the most enjoyable activities on the earth is eating with others. Friends eat together, families eat together, people interested in one another eat together, strangers eat together to get to know one another. As we eat with others, it often increases our enjoyment of the food.
Proverbs 13:20 says, "He who walks with the wise becomes wise, but the friend of fools will suffer harm" (paraphrase). Wisdom and foolishness in Scripture are not intellectual issues but spiritual issues. The fool says in his heart there is no God (Ps 14:1).

Therefore, the wise are those who love, honor, and obey God. By walking with the wise, we will become wise. If we walk with those who love and study God's Word, it will increase our love and knowledge of the Word. If we walk with those passionate about evangelism, the spirit of evangelism will catch fire in our hearts.

However, the opposite is true as well. If we walk with those who are disobedient to God or who compromise their faith, we will do the same. It is often said that friends of the same feather flock together. Often our closes friends will be people like us—either people who desperately hunger for God and the things of God or people who lack spiritual hunger.

Which are you? Are you helping cultivate hunger for God in those around you? Or are you putting out their fire by your compromise?

Application Question: How is God calling you to pursue a healthier appetite? Are there any other ways believers can cultivate a healthy appetite?

The Promise to the Hungry

> Blessed are those who hunger and thirst for righteousness for they will be satisfied.
> Matthew 5:6

This promise seems to have two aspects:

1. God promises to fill the hungry with righteousness.

The word "satisfy" can also be translated "fill" (NIV). Essentially, this means that our righteousness is proportional to our spiritual appetite. Those who hunger for God's Word—God reveals it to them in deeper ways. Those who hunger for souls—God gives them disciples. Those who hunger to serve—God provides opportunities. Therefore, those who don't hunger lack righteousness.

It has been those who desperately hungered for righteousness throughout history that God used the most. It was not the wisest or most talented. It was those that hungered. John Knox, who God greatly used to stir revival in Scotland, once said, "Give me Scotland or I die!" He was somebody who desperately hungered and thirsted, and God greatly used him as a result.

Are you desperately hungry for righteousness in your life and others? If so, God will fill it. If not, you will lack righteousness.

2. God promises to satisfy the hungry.

There is an emotional component to the word "satisfy." Most are never satisfied because they pursue contentment in possessions, fame, power, and love. However, only righteousness can truly satisfy us—only knowing God and serving him and others. Anything else will leave us dry, both in this life and throughout eternity.

Application Question: In what ways have you experienced hunger for righteousness and God satisfying that hunger? In what ways have you experienced lack when you haven't hungered?

Conclusion

Appetite is an indicator of our physical health, and it's the same with our spiritual health. God smiles on and approves of those who desperately hunger and thirst for righteousness. They hunger for a more intimate relationship with God, a deeper knowledge of God's Word, the salvation of the lost, and ultimately, God's will to be done in every situation. Because they hunger and thirst, God fills and satisfies them. And one day, they will ultimately be satisfied with God's presence and perfect righteousness in heaven.

Are you still hungering and thirsting for righteousness? If so, God promises to fill those desires.

Blessed Are the Merciful

> Blessed are the merciful, for they will be shown mercy.
> Matthew 5:7 (NET)

As mentioned previously, the Beatitudes are character traits of those who have entered the kingdom of heaven (cf. Matt 5:3, 10). We have learned that believers are the poor in spirit—they recognize their lack of righteousness before God. This leads them to mourn over their sin. They become the meek—those who humble themselves and submit to God's control. This leads them to the fifth beatitude—hunger for righteousness and the promise of God filling that hunger. This is a turning point in the Beatitudes. The first four are inner character changes that reflect the believer's relationship with God; the last four are outward manifestations of those character changes, which reflect the believer's relationship with others.[32] As believers hunger for righteousness, God makes them the merciful (5:7), the pure in heart (5:8), and the peacemakers (5:9). Because of this righteousness, the world persecutes them (5:10).

In this study, we will consider the fifth beatitude, "Blessed are the merciful, for they will be shown mercy."

Big Question: What does the fifth beatitude mean and how should it be applied?

The Merciful

Interpretation Question: What is mercy? What is the difference between mercy and grace?

Mercy is goodness offered to those in misery or distress. It often includes compassion or forbearance shown to an offender—somebody that deserves only justice. John MacArthur defines it as follows:

> Mercy is meeting people's needs. It is not simply feeling compassion but showing compassion, not only sympathizing but giving a helping hand. Mercy is giving food to the hungry, comfort to the bereaved, love to the rejected, forgiveness to the offender, companionship to the lonely. It is therefore one of the loveliest and noblest of all virtues.[33]

Scripture teaches us that God is merciful. Paul called God the "Father of mercies and the God of all comfort" (2 Cor 1:3). Psalm 103:8 says, "The Lord is merciful and gracious" (ESV). In Titus 3:5, Paul states that God saved us not because of our righteous deeds but because of his mercy. Hebrews 2:17 calls Christ our merciful high priest. The believer is merciful because God is merciful. When a person becomes born again, God's mercy begins to manifest through his life in various ways. In fact, it will identify him.

Now it should be said that this concept—the very idea of mercy—was radical to the Roman world. Mercy was despised by Romans. MacArthur adds:

> A popular Roman philosopher called mercy "the disease of the soul." It was the supreme sign of weakness. Mercy was a sign that you did not have what it takes to be a real man and especially a real Roman. The Romans glorified manly courage, strict justice, firm discipline, and, above all, absolute power. They looked down on mercy, because mercy to them was weakness, and weakness was despised above all other human limitations.[34]

Though at times despised or considered weak by the world, mercy is a supreme virtue since it is a character trait of both God and his people.

We must ask, "What is the difference between mercy and grace?" These terms are often used synonymously; however, they are slightly different. *Grace is unmerited favor to those who don't deserve it. Mercy is unmerited favor towards the miserable or hurting.* It often includes withholding justice others deserve.

Application Question: In what ways should believers show mercy to others?

1. Believers show mercy by helping those caught in desperate circumstances.

This is emphasized in both the Old Testament and New Testament. Israel was commanded to take care of foreigners because they once were foreigners in Egypt (Lev 19:34). They were called to not harvest the sides of their fields, as they should be left for the poor (Lev 23:22). They were also called to care for the widow and the orphan and not oppress them. Zechariah 7:9-10 orders, "The LORD who rules over all said, 'Exercise true judgment and show brotherhood and compassion to each other. You must not oppress the widow, the orphan, the foreigner, or the poor, nor should anyone secretly plot evil against his fellow human being.'"

Similarly, James wrote to scattered Christians saying: "Pure and undefiled religion before God the Father is this: to care for orphans and widows in their misfortune and to keep oneself unstained by the world" (Jam 1:27). Like Israel before them, the early church focused on caring for those in desperate circumstances. When Paul and Barnabas were sent to the Gentiles by the apostles, they were asked to "remember the poor" (Gal 2:10).

Mercy was perfectly manifested in Christ. His ministry was primarily to the despised and downtrodden. He healed the sick and fed the poor. Christ declared this about himself in Luke 4:18-19:

> "The Spirit of the Lord is upon me, because he has anointed me to proclaim good news to the poor. He has sent me to proclaim release to the captives and the regaining of sight to the blind, to set free those who are oppressed, to proclaim the year of the Lord's favor."

In Acts 2:45, the early church sold all they had and gave to the poor among them. As followers of Christ, we must also care for the poor, sick, struggling, and oppressed. We should be zealous about this ministry as well. It is our Christian duty. Those who are part of the kingdom will be greatly involved in these ministries. They are the merciful.

Darren Carlson, the President of Training Leader's International, shared this about his conversation with refugees while visiting Christians in Athens:

> I can't tell you how many times, I have heard this from Iranian and Afghan believers:
>
> *I left my country, and everywhere on my way to Greece, there were Christians. As I left my country, Muslims were literally shooting at me and my family. But in Turkey and Greece, Christians have welcomed me, clothed me, and fed me. When I got off the boat, it was Christians that were passing out food and water. When I came to Athens, it was Christians who gave me a shower, helped me with a medical issue, and gave me a meal with spices from my home. I became a Christian because they were so different than Muslims.*

Caring for those in miserable circumstances must be the ethic and practice of Christians. Are you reaching out to the poor, needy, and desperate, as our Lord did?

2. Believers show mercy by helping those caught in sin.

Obviously, Christ perfectly displayed this as well. He came to save people from their sin. He told the woman caught in adultery and a cripple that he healed to sin no more (John 8:11, 5:14). He called people to repent, turn from their sin, and follow him. Ultimately, he delivers all who turn to him from the penalty and power of sin, and one day, he will deliver them from the presence of sin.

Followers of Christ should help people struggling with sin as well. Galatians 6:1-2 says,

> Brothers and sisters, if a person is discovered in some sin, you who are spiritual restore such a person in a spirit of gentleness. Pay close attention to yourselves, so that you are not tempted too. Carry one another's burdens, and in this way you will fulfill the law of Christ.

How should we help those caught in sin? By using Scripture, we should lovingly correct other believers by showing them how they are thinking and acting incorrectly. Then, again by using Scripture, we should show them how to get right with God and help hold them accountable (cf. 2 Tim 3:16-17).

Mercy towards sinners does not only include helping believers get right with God, but it also includes helping unbelievers turn from their sin to follow Christ. Sharing the Gospel is the most merciful act we can do, and every believer should participate in this ministry.

Are you being merciful by lovingly correcting believers and sharing the Gospel with the lost?

3. Believers show mercy by forgiving those who sinned against them.

Colossians 3:13 says, "bearing with one another and forgiving one another, if someone happens to have a complaint against anyone else. Just as the Lord has forgiven you, so you also forgive others." The command to forgive as Christ forgave should turn us away from shallow attempts at forgiveness. Many declare, "I forgive you, but I don't ever want to see you or talk to you again." However, that is not how God forgives us. Scripture says God remembers our sins no more (Is 43:25). This doesn't mean that God can forget; he can't, since he is omniscient. It means that he no longer holds our sins against us as a barrier to intimacy or usefulness. We must do the same. This doesn't mean that we don't recognize people's immaturity, propensity to bend the truth, or hurt us. It just means that we love them through those events and issues, and aim to help them grow in holiness—which may include things like correction, discipline, and times of separation (cf. Matt 18:15-17, 1 Cor 5:9-13).

Are you forgiving those who have failed you?

Application Question: What is your experience with mercy ministries, such as caring for orphans, widows, and the poor, as well as correcting those in sin and sharing the Gospel? What makes mercy ministries both difficult and enriching?

The Promise to the Merciful

Interpretation Question: What does God's promise to the merciful mean practically—"blessed are the merciful for they will be shown mercy"?

1. God's promise means that God will help the merciful in times of need.

Proverbs 19:17 says, "The one who is gracious to the poor lends to the Lord, and the Lord will repay him for his good deed." In Matthew 6:1-3, Christ talks about God's reward for those who give to the needy with right hearts, which includes heavenly reward (cf. Matt 6:19). In 2 Corinthians 9:7-8, Paul declares that if we are cheerful givers, God will provide grace to meet all our needs and to excel in good works. Verse 8 says, "And God is able to make all grace overflow to you so that because you have enough of everything in every way at all times, you will overflow in every good work." The promise of mercy applies both to our practical and spiritual needs. If we excel at mercy, God will not only provide for our financial needs but open doors for greater service. God blesses those who are channels—not reservoirs.

Similarly, Malachi 3:10-12 says:

> "Bring the entire tithe into the storehouse so that there may be food in my temple. Test me in this matter," says the LORD who rules over all, "to see if I will not open for you the windows of heaven and pour out for you a blessing until there is no room for it all. Then I will stop the plague from ruining your crops, and the vine will not lose its fruit before harvest," says the LORD who rules over all. "All nations will call you happy, for you indeed will live in a delightful land," says the LORD who rules over all.

The tithe was used to take care of the temple, provide for the needs of the priests and Levites, and feed the poor. God promised that if his people excelled in giving tithes, he would open the heavens and bless them with something so large they wouldn't be able to receive it. Because of God's blessing, all the nations would call Israel blessed.

Likewise, when believers give abundantly to church ministries, mission and mercy organizations, and the needy, they spiritually and practically enrich themselves. Luke 6:38 says, "Give, and it will be given to you: A good measure, pressed down, shaken together, running over, will be poured into your lap. For the measure you use will be the measure you receive.'" Psalm 41:1-3 says:

> How blessed is the one who treats the poor properly! When trouble comes, the LORD delivers him. May the LORD protect him and save his life! May he be blessed in the land! Do not turn him over to his enemies! The LORD

supports him on his sickbed; you completely heal him from his illness.

2. God's promise implies that God will discipline believers for their lack of mercy.

Proverbs 28:27 says, "The one who gives to the poor will not lack, but whoever shuts his eyes to them will receive many curses." These curses don't just come from a lack of giving but a lack of mercy in general. In Matthew 6:14-15, we see how God disciplines those who don't forgive others. It says, "For if you forgive others their sins, your heavenly Father will also forgive you. But if you do not forgive others, your Father will not forgive you your sins."

This discipline is clearly demonstrated in the Parable of the Merciless Servant (Matt 18). In the parable, a master forgives a servant a great debt—the equivalent of twenty million in U.S. currency. Yes, immediately after this, the servant refuses to forgive his fellow servant a small debt of roughly two thousand dollars in today's currency.[35] Because of this, the master throws the unforgiving servant into jail to be tortured until the original debt was paid. In Matthew 18:35, Christ said this to his disciples, "So also my heavenly Father will do to you, if each of you does not forgive your brother from your heart." This discipline shows up in many ways: trials, demonic attacks, sickness, etc. (cf. 1 Cor 5:5, 11:21-22, 30-31). James 2:13 reminds us that, "For judgment is merciless for the one who has shown no mercy."

Unforgiveness and a lack of mercy in general hinder our intimacy with God and also bring harsh discipline.

3. God's promise implies that lacking mercy proves that we've never received mercy and therefore lack salvation.

Some have misinterpreted this beatitude to mean that we can earn salvation by being merciful. However, this doesn't take into account the context of the Beatitudes. As mentioned, there is a progression. The first four Beatitudes are inner changes in believers which begin at salvation and continue throughout sanctification. Then there are outer manifestations of these inner changes in the next four. In addition, the interpretation of mercy as a way of earning salvation clearly contradicts Scripture's teaching that salvation is by faith alone—apart from works (cf. Gen 15:6, Eph 2:8-9). Though not a means of salvation, practicing mercy is both a fruit and proof of salvation. It provides believers with assurance of whether they possess saving faith or not.

This assurance manifests itself in two tests: First, if we are unmerciful to the needs of the world, then we are not saved. First John 3:17 says: "But whoever has the world's possessions and sees his fellow Christian in need and shuts off his compassion against him, how can the love of God reside in such a person?" Additionally, in the Parable of the Sheep and the Goats, Christ said this to the goats:

> "Then he will say to those on his left, 'Depart from me, you accursed, into the eternal fire that has been prepared for the devil and his angels! For I was hungry and you gave me nothing to eat, I was thirsty and you gave me nothing to drink. I was a stranger and you did not receive me as a guest, naked and you did not clothe me, sick and in prison and you did not visit me.'
> Matthew 25:41-43

Their lack of mercy proved their lack of salvation. God's love had never changed their selfish hearts (cf. Rom 5:5); they lived to serve only themselves, not God and others.

Secondly, if we are unforgiving and vengeful towards those who hurt us, this may demonstrate that we have never received mercy. For it is those who have been shown mercy who will constantly show mercy to others. This doesn't mean that if we struggle at times to forgive others or show mercy that we're not saved. It means that if there is no struggle—that is, if we are just vengeful, unforgiving, and unconcerned about the desperate needs of others—then we are not born again.

Are you the merciful? Or are you unforgiving and unconcerned about the pains of others?

Application Question: How have you experienced a change in your life towards being more merciful as you've grown in Christ? In what ways have you experienced God's promise either for showing mercy or neglecting to show it?

Growth in the Practice of Mercy

Application Question: How can we grow in the practice of mercy?

1. To grow in the practice of mercy, we must remember our own sin and desperate situation.

This is often what we don't do. We see how others have failed us, but we forget that we have both failed God and others. We consider how stupid and inconsiderate someone else is, but forget times in our past when we were stupid and inconsiderate. We condemn the person who cut us off in traffic and yet forget that we've made mistakes in driving as well. Forgetting our own sins and failures leads to harshness in judging others. It is sin nature to emphasize our goodness and minimize our badness. In fact, we tend to condemn others as a means of building ourselves up. We say to ourselves (and often others), "I can't believe they did that!" "I could do that better." or "I would never do that!" Like the Pharisees, we primarily see our successes and not our failures— leading us to condemn others when they fail (cf. Lk 18:9-14). The Pharisees were unmerciful because they thought themselves to be so righteous.

However, it is the one who deeply mourns over his sin that is truly merciful (cf. Matt 5:4, 7). It has been said that, "Unless we recognize ourselves as chief of sinners, like Paul (1 Tim 1:15), we are not yet ready for ministry." Unless we have become like Isaiah, who declared that he was deserving of judgment because of the sins of his mouth, we are not ready to be sent, like him, to serve those caught in sin (Is 6). If we don't recognize our own great depravity, we will not be gentle or effective in our ministry to others. We will not be the merciful. In fact, we may be abusive.

Are you remembering your failures? You can tell by whether your response is typically gentle or harsh when others fail you.

Application Question: In what ways have you experienced yourself being overly harsh with others and their failures, especially with areas you previously struggled with? How have you seen this hypocritical spirit in others? How can we grow in awareness of our sins?

2. To grow in the practice of mercy, we must identify with others.

An aspect of mercy is sympathy and compassion. It is identifying with others' pain and struggles. It is seeing through their eyes and walking with their feet. When we truly do this, we will work to alleviate their pain, and we'll also forgive their misgivings. This is exactly how Christ sought to provide mercy for us. He didn't stay in heaven and simply watch our pain and failures. He came down and became human. He felt and experienced poverty. He experienced the loss of a father at an early age. He was mocked, betrayed, and hurt. Though he never sinned, he experienced temptation and bore our sins on the cross. He identified with us so he could deliver us and forgive us.

This is the very reason why many don't show mercy. We don't want to see through the eyes and experiences of others. We want to help, but we don't want to taste their cup of suffering. It is when touching the leper, sitting beside the person dying in the hospice, living with the poor, and eating and drinking with the lost that true compassion is developed. It is as we identify with the hurting and lost that true mercy—compassion in action—is fostered.

I experienced this while working with people with developmental needs for three years. Essentially, I was a house parent: I gave them their medications, prepared breakfast for them, bathed and shaved them, counseled them, and was available to them at night if anything went wrong. Before I started working with this population, I remember being hesitant and a little scared. I was scared simply because I had never really been around people with such special needs. Theologically, I knew my hesitancy was wrong, but practically, it was still there. However, when I started working with them, I fell in love with them. They became some of my closest friends. I loved talking and hanging out with them; eventually, they started coming to church with me. But, it wasn't until I started living with them and serving them, that my heart started to grow for them. By identifying with them, a desire to alleviate their pain grew in me.

This is why believers are often radically changed by going on a mission trip or serving in a mercy ministry. By touching the broken, as our Lord did, their hearts are radically changed. They start to sympathize and work for their deliverance.

This is also true with forgiveness. It is the past experiences of others that lead them to act as they do, including hurting others. As people start to really consider the paths others have walked, in order to empathize with them, it becomes easier to forgive their failures. There is a French proverb that says, "to understand all is to forgive all." In addition, it has often been said, "Hurt people, hurt people." By understanding the hurts of those who hurt and fail us, it will be easier to forgive them.

Have you developed compassion for the hurting? Are you identifying with them?

Application Question: Why is identifying with others so important not only for mercy ministry but ministry in general? In what ways have you experienced the importance of identifying with others as the one receiving mercy or giving it?

3. To grow in the practice of mercy, we must develop our love for others.

God does not just want people to give or to help others in pain. He wants them to do it with the right heart—one full of love.

Paul said, "If I give all my possessions to the poor and don't have love, I gain nothing" (1 Cor 13:10, paraphrase). He also said we should not give out of necessity or compulsion for God loves a cheerful giver (2 Cor 9:7). God wants believers to be just like him. He wants us to love serving and giving.

Micah 6:8 says: "He has showed you, O man, what is good. And what does the LORD require of you? To act justly and to love mercy and to walk humbly with your God" (NIV 1984). Micah says we must not only show mercy but love it. It is very possible for our acts of kindness and forgiveness toward others to stem from wrong motives, including simply being done out of obligation. First Peter 4:9 instructs us to "Show hospitality to one another without complaining."

This is important to hear because people who serve in mercy ministries tend to struggle with bitterness and burn-out; the work is hard and the people are often difficult and ungracious. Even Christ was hated by the people he served. Mercy ministers will constantly experience criticism, attacks, and a lack of gratefulness from those they serve as well. It can be hard to keep a right heart at times.

However, God not only commands our actions, but he commands our hearts. He commands us to love him with all our heart, mind, and soul and to love our neighbors as ourselves (Mk 12:30-31). He calls us to give thanks in all circumstances for this is God's will for our lives (1 Thess 5:18). Also, through living in the Holy Spirit, he provides us with the fruit of love, patience, perseverance, and self-control (Gal 5:16, 22-23). He will give us grace to be merciful and do it with the right heart.

Do you love showing mercy? Or is it simply an obligation? As we show mercy, we must have the right heart—one filled with love.

Application Question: Why is it so common for those serving in mercy ministries to become bitter and lose a right heart? In what ways have you experienced hurt from those you served? How did you overcome it or remain faithful? How can we grow to love mercy?

4. To grow in the practice of mercy, we must remember God's promise to the merciful.

Proverbs 11:25 (NIV) says, "A generous person will prosper; whoever refreshes others will be refreshed." God promises to bless and refresh those who serve others. When Christ was burnt out, God refreshed him with the ministry of angels (Mark 1:13). When Elijah was weary, God refreshed him with food brought by ravens (1 Kings 19:3-6). When David was weary, he "drew strength from the Lord" (1 Sam 30:6). This promise brings encouragement especially when we, as ministers, feel like quitting or giving up. God promises to bless and refresh us.

This also should be an encouragement to those too depressed or discouraged to serve. Sometimes, the best way to receive encouragement or relief is to show mercy to others; for then, God will show mercy to us. Christ promised that by taking on his yoke of service, we will find rest for our souls (Matt 11:29). God's promise is a tremendous motivation to practice the ministry of mercy.

Application Question: In what ways have you experienced God's refreshment in ministry? Is there anybody that you feel God wants you to encourage and refresh for their faithful ministry efforts? In what ways is God calling you to pursue growth in mercy and seek his promise to the merciful?

Conclusion

Christ is our merciful high priest (Heb 2:17). He identified with us, as he came down to this world as a man. He preached the good news to the poor. He set free captives of sin and the devil. He fed the hungry and healed the sick. He died for our sins, and therefore was the perfect manifestation of mercy. If he lives in us, his characteristic of mercy should manifest in some way, no matter how small, in our lives. Blessed are the merciful for they (and they alone) shall receive mercy. Are you growing in mercy?

Blessed Are the Pure in Heart

> Blessed are the pure in heart, for they will see God.
> Matthew 5:8 (NET)

As a reminder, the fourth beatitude, hungering and thirsting for righteousness, marked a pivot in the Beatitudes. From there, God begins to fill his people with righteousness. He makes them the merciful, the pure in heart, and the peacemakers. In many ways, "Blessed are the pure in heart, for they shall see God" is the chief beatitude. Some have wondered why it is not the first beatitude or the last, as the culmination.[36] Throughout history, seeing and knowing God has often been considered the summum bonum—the highest good in life. Jeremiah quotes the Lord:

> Let not the wise boast of their wisdom or the strong boast of their strength or the rich boast of their riches, but let the one who boasts boast about this: that they have the understanding to know me
> Jeremiah 9:23-24 (NIV)

He names three things that people often pursue in life as the highest good: wisdom, strength, and wealth; however, the highest good is knowing God. This is essentially what Matthew 5:8 promises—to see and know God more intimately.

Moses cried out for this in Exodus 33:18, as he asked to see God's glory. God responded to him that no one could see his face and live. However, he would show Moses his back—a manifestation of his glory, but not his full glory. Here in Matthew 5:8, Christ promises the highest good that man can achieve—seeing and knowing God. It is for this reason that some view this beatitude as the climax or pinnacle of the Beatitudes; the first five lead to it and the last two flow from it.[37]

In this study, we'll consider the sixth beatitude: the blessing on the pure in heart and the promise of seeing God.

Big Question: What does the sixth beatitude mean and what applications can we take from it?

The Pure in Heart

Interpretation Question: What does it mean to be pure in heart?

The word "pure" has had a variety of uses: It was used of soiled clothes which had been washed clean, and an army of soldiers which had been purged of the discontented, unwilling, cowardly, and inefficient soldiers—with only first-class fighters remaining.[38] It was also used of metals that had been refined until all the impurities were gone—leaving only pure silver, pure gold, etc.[39] Therefore, the word generally means both "clean" and "unmixed."

When Christ adds the word "heart" to it, he is not just referring to emotions. In the biblical mindset, "heart" refers to the mind, will, and emotions.[40] Therefore, we must ask what does Christ mean practically by being "pure in heart"?

1. To be pure in heart refers to having an inner moral righteousness.

When people follow God and are born again, God begins to change their hearts. He starts ridding them of jealousy, anger, pride, and selfishness, and replacing these attitudes with selflessness, humility, love, patience, and other virtues. The more a person grows in these godly virtues, the more they see God. Therefore, to hold on to ungodly attitudes is to hinder our relationship with God and our ability to see him. We see this commonly in Scripture. James 1:7-8 describes how the double-minded man is unstable in all his ways and how he will receive nothing from God when he prays. The double-minded man is somebody who wants to live for the world and live for God at the same time (cf. James 4:3-4). Therefore, he is unstable and ineffective in prayer. Likewise, David said if he cherished iniquity in his heart, the Lord would not hear him (Ps 66:18). To love sin, to cultivate unforgiveness, or pride is to hinder our relationship with God and our ability to see him.

This was especially important for the Jews and Pharisees to hear, as they tended to focus on outward compliance to God's laws instead of inward compliance. They thought if they hadn't killed anyone, they had kept the law against murder, but Christ said to be angry is to commit murder in our hearts. They thought if they hadn't committed adultery, they had kept that commandment, but Christ said to lust is to commit adultery. To commit either of these is to fail to both love God and man, which are the greatest commandments. Christ rebuked the Pharisees for this by calling them white-washed tombs—clean on the outside but filled with dead men's bones on the inside (Matt 23:27). He described them as drawing near God with their mouths while their hearts were far from him (Matt 15:8). Clearly, the Pharisees didn't give attention to cultivating pure hearts.

Psalm 24:3-4 (NIV) says, "Who may ascend the mountain of the LORD? Who may stand in his holy place? The one who has clean hands and a pure heart, who does not trust in an idol or swear by a false god." This Psalm seems to describe the ideal worshiper. "Clean hands" refers to godly works, and a "pure heart" refers to inner morality. When our heart is right, it leads to right actions. This is the person that God allows into his presence. He seeks after worshipers, who worship him in spirit (heart) and truth (John 4:23).

Are you developing an inner morality? If so, you will increasingly see God. The more you cultivate honesty, integrity, patience, perseverance, hatred for sin, etc., the more you will experience God's presence.

2. To be pure in heart refers to being sincere—free of hypocrisy.

This is certainly part of inner morality, but worth separating for emphasis. As we continue to study the Sermon on the Mount, and the Gospels in general, Christ will repeatedly mention this. In Matthew 6, he calls for the disciples to not be like the Pharisees and teachers of the law who did their acts of righteousness (praying, giving, and fasting) to be seen by men. He says if we do this, then we have received our reward—the acknowledgment of men—but we will not be rewarded by God.

This is something those who serve in ministry must be particularly aware of. It is easy to start to do good works for the applause of men. We can tell if this is in our hearts by how we respond when criticized or praised by others; criticism will overly discourage us, and praise will overly excite us. Are we really seeking God's honor and praise alone? It is also possible to do good works primarily for financial purposes. Christ stressed that he was the good shepherd and all who came before him were just hirelings—doing ministry simply for pay. When the wolf comes, the hireling flees because he is only there for pay (John 10). How do we respond when we encounter trials in our ministry—our service to God and others? If we are just there for the benefits, we will not stay committed.

Are our motives for serving God pure? Or are they mixed and insincere?

3. To be pure in heart refers to being single-minded in devotion to God.

As mentioned, the word "pure" was used of cleansing an army—getting rid of the cowardly and the uncommitted and leaving only the most devoted and effective fighters. Sadly, we are often like this with God—divided between love for the world and its things, and love for God and his kingdom. Therefore, many Christians are stunted in their growth. They are not hearing God's voice, not enjoying his presence, because this is something God gives to the single-minded—the devoted. Matthew 13:22 describes how "worldly cares and the seductiveness of wealth choke the word, so it produces nothing." It's the divided heart that misses God's best.

In Philippians 3:13 (NIV), Paul said, "this one thing I do"—referring to his pursuit of knowing and being rewarded by Christ (cf. v. 10-12, 14). Sadly, for most, God is just one of their many things, and therefore, they miss out on a heightened intimacy with God. Through Jeremiah, God said this to the idolatrous Israelites who were deported to Babylon, "When you seek me in prayer and worship, you will find me available to you. If you seek me with all your heart and soul" (Jer 29:13). It is when we turn away from our idols and come after God with our whole heart that we will truly see him and know him.

Are you pursuing God with your whole heart or are you half-hearted?

Application Question: Which aspect of purity of heart stood out to you most and why (inner morality, sincerity, single-minded devotion)? What are common idols that distract people from single-minded devotion to God? Describe a season (or seasons) in your life when you were the most single-minded. What contributed to your passion and devotion? What eventually detracted from it?

Growth in Purity of Heart

Application Question: How can we grow in purity of heart?

1. To grow in purity of heart, we must make sure that we are saved.

It is the pure in heart, and they alone, who will see God. As with the other beatitudes, these characteristics are only true of the born again. Hebrews 12:14 says without holiness "no one will see the Lord." What God does at salvation is give us a clean heart—a new nature. It is a promise of the New Covenant. Ezekiel 36:25-26 says,

"'I will take you from the nations and gather you from all the countries; then I will bring you to your land. I will sprinkle you with pure water and you will be clean from all your impurities. I will purify you from all your idols. I will give you a new heart, and I will put a new spirit within you. I will remove the heart of stone from your body and give you a heart of flesh.

At salvation, purity of heart begins; God gives us a new nature and new desires—desires to pursue him and obey him. This is one of the ways that we know that we are saved. We know something of purity of heart—singleness of mind—a desire to follow Christ as Lord and please him above ourselves and everybody else.

Have you experienced this new heart?

2. To grow in purity of heart, we must continually confess anything unpleasing to God.

While on earth, we will never be completely pure of heart. Jeremiah 17:9 says that our hearts are "deceitful above all things and beyond cure" (paraphrase) and yet, Christ still commands us: "be perfect, as your heavenly father is perfect" (Matt 5:48). Consequently, we must continually confess pride, anger, lust, and everything that dishonors God. In fact, we must ask God to help us discern the evil in our hearts, as we often are blind to its defects. In Psalm 139:23-24, David prays, "Examine me, and probe my thoughts! Test me, and know my concerns! See if there is any idolatrous tendency in me, and lead me in the reliable ancient path!" As we discern wrong attitudes and actions, we must confess and repent to God. When we do this, God is faithful and just to forgive us and cleanse us from all unrighteousness (1 John 1:9).

Are you daily confessing and repenting of wrong attitudes, words, and actions?

3. To grow in purity of heart, we must guard and protect our hearts.

Our hearts are idol factories—prone to love and worship things other than God. Because of this, we must continually guard it, not only from sinful things but also good things that might steal our affections. Proverbs 4:23 says, "Guard your heart with all vigilance, for from it are the sources of life." In Matthew 6:19-21, Christ, aware of this sinful tendency in our hearts, commanded believers to not store up riches on this earth, not because riches are inherently sinful, but because wherever our riches are, our hearts will be also. Riches tend to steal our hearts from God and seeking his kingdom first. We must be aware of this disease in our hearts—they are prone to love entertainment, clothes, cars, career, social media, popularity, etc., over God. For some of us, we must forsake certain possessions, even as Christ commanded the rich man (Matt 19:16-22). We can't handle them appropriately; they will keep us out of the Word, away from prayer, and serving God. For others, we will just have to be disciplined in our use of these objects. This is a wisdom principle; each believer will have to discern this through the Holy Spirit and the counsel of godly saints. What might be a treasure (and therefore a temptation) to one person, might not be a treasure for another.

4. To grow in purity of heart, we must pray for it.

In prayer, we recognize that only God can truly change our hearts. In Psalm 51:10, David prayed: "Create for me a pure heart, O God! Renew a resolute spirit within me!" *Create in me a heart that is solely devoted to you—one that beats to honor your name and build your kingdom.* We must recognize our lack of a clean heart and cry out for it. In Psalm 86:11 (NIV), David again prayed, "Give me an undivided heart, that I may fear your name." *So many things pull me away from you, unify my mind to worship you, Lord.* If we are going to grow in purity of heart, like David, we must cry out for it.

5. To grow in purity of heart, we must saturate ourselves with God's Word.

Christ said this to his disciples in John 15:3, "You are clean already because of the word that I have spoken to you." It was through hearing the Gospel and believing it, that the disciples were made clean, as Christ gave them new hearts. However, it is still through God's Word that our hearts are daily made clean. Hebrews 4:12 says, "For the word of God is living and active and sharper than any double-edged sword, piercing even to the point of dividing soul from spirit, and joints from marrow; it is able to judge the desires and thoughts of the heart."

As we study God's Word, it cuts us. It reveals wrong heart motives and makes us more into the image of Christ. It sanctifies us.

Are you living in God's Word?

6. To grow in purity of heart, we must desire the promise of knowing God more than anything else.

If you really desire to see God more and more, then you will be willing to get rid of anything that corrupts your heart. Is it your entertainment—your music and TV watching—that defiles your heart with explicit content? If so, you must be willing to get rid of it to know God more. Is it your relationships that are drawing you away from Christ? If so, you must be willing to let go of them to know God more. If you don't really want to see God and experience him, then you won't do whatever it takes to be pure in heart.

Philippians 4:8-9 (NIV) says,

> Finally, brothers and sisters, whatever is true, whatever is noble, whatever is right, whatever is pure, whatever is lovely, whatever is admirable—if anything is excellent or praiseworthy—think about such things. Whatever you have learned or received or heard from me, or seen in me—put it into practice. And the God of peace will be with you.

To think on what is noble, right, pure, and lovely, we must, by necessity, let go of what is common, wrong, compromised, and ugly. It is only when our thoughts and practices are right, that the God of peace will be with us, as we experience his presence and intimacy in a special way.

7. To grow in purity of heart, we must continually think on eternity.

   First John 3:2-3 says,

   Dear friends, we are God's children now, and what we will be has not yet been revealed. We know that whenever it is revealed we will be like him, because we will see him just as he is. And everyone who has this hope focused on him purifies himself, just as Jesus is pure).

   The more we hope to see and serve Christ throughout eternity, the more we will want to purify ourselves because we want to please him. However, if our hearts are continually set on this world and the things of the world, we will become increasingly secular and worldly—dimming our spiritual sight.

   Are you thinking on eternity and seeing Christ?

Application Question: What are some other practices that aid in developing purity of heart? In what ways is God challenging you to pursue growth in purity of heart?

Seeing God

Interpretation Question: What does the promise of seeing God mean?

1. Seeing God has a present aspect to it.

- Believers will see God in creation.

In Psalm 19:1-2, David said that the heavens declare the glory of God and that they daily pour forth speech about him. In Psalm 29:7-10, David describes seeing and experiencing God in a thunder storm:

> The Lord's shout strikes with flaming fire. The Lord's shout shakes the wilderness, the Lord shakes the wilderness of Kadesh. The Lord's shout bends the large trees and strips the leaves from the forests. Everyone in his temple says, "Majestic! The Lord sits enthroned over the engulfing waters, the Lord sits enthroned as the eternal king.

David, a man after God's own heart, even saw God in his imperfect and aging body, as he declared how he was fearfully and wonderfully made (Ps 139:14). Only the pure in heart have this type of sight. They see God even in imperfect things like creation, as it still bears his marks. Similarly, when the disciples were fearful about their futures, Christ comforted them with God's work in creation (Matt 6). He asked, "Did you see the lilies of the field today—how God clothed them? Did you see the birds of the air—how God fed them?" Christ saw creation as revealing God's love and providence. As we grow in purity of heart, we'll see God more in his creation.

- Believers see God in difficult circumstances.

We saw this with Joseph. After his father died, his brothers pleaded with him to not treat them harshly. Joseph responded, "As for you, you meant to harm me, but God intended it for a good purpose, so he could preserve the lives of many people, as you can see this day" (Gen 50:20). He saw God's goodness in the storms of life where others might have doubted God, became angry at him, or turned away from him. We also saw this with Job—even after he had lost his family and much of his business—he declared, "The Lord gives, and the Lord takes away.

May the name of the Lord be blessed!" (Job 1:21). To him, both blessings and trials came from the hand of God. When Stephen was stoned, Christ appeared to him in the clouds—no doubt strengthening him to be the church's first martyr (Acts 7:56). God works all things to the good of those who love the Lord, including trials (Rom 8:28).

Are you seeing his hand in your trials?

- Believers see God in acts of worship.

The purer our hearts, the more we will see and experience God, as we study God's Word, pray, fellowship with others, and serve. When our hearts are not pure, we will meditate on Scripture and receive nothing. We will worship and pray, but it's as if the heavens are shut. We'll serve, and it will only be a burden. God reveals himself to those with right hearts.

2. Seeing God has a future aspect.

Obviously, we will most clearly see God in heaven. First Corinthians 13:12 says, "For now we see in a mirror indirectly, but then we will see face to face. Now I know in part, but then I will know fully, just as I have been fully known." This verse compares our vision of God to looking into a mirror. Ancient mirrors were made of polished stone or metal and therefore weren't very clear—the reflection was dim at best. However, in eternity, we will see God face to face. We will know him, even as he knows us. This is the great hope of believers. Only those who are truly born again will ultimately see God.

Application Question: In what ways have you experienced the promise of seeing and experiencing God when your heart was pure before God? In what ways have you experienced a lack of intimacy with God when in sin or consumed with lesser things?

Conclusion

"Blessed are the pure in heart" is the climax of the Beatitudes. It is the climax because it brings the greatest blessing—seeing God. As seeing and knowing God becomes our highest pursuit in life, there will be no cost that we are unwilling to pay, and no height that we are unwilling to climb to know him. Blessed are the pure in heart for they, and they alone, will see God. Lord, purify our hearts. Amen.

Blessed Are the Peacemakers

> Blessed are the peacemakers, for they will be called the children of God.
> Matthew 5:9 (NET)

As Christ continues his lesson on the characteristics of believers, it is no surprise that after speaking on the "pure in heart" that he now focuses on the peacemakers. It is only those who daily conquer sin in their own lives—who work to bring peace to the civil war in their own hearts—that are ready to help others fight this battle as well.

Peacemakers are those who mourn over sin, those who purify their lives, and help others do the same. This does not make them popular. In fact, it often leads to persecution, as we'll see in the next beatitude: "Blessed are those who are persecuted for righteousness" (Matt 5:10). However, this ministry is needed.

In this study, we will consider what it means to be a peacemaker, how to grow in our peacemaking, and the reward of peacemakers.

Big Question: What does the seventh beatitude mean and what are some applications we can take from it?

Peacemakers

Interpretation Question: What does it mean to be a peacemaker?

"Peace" or "Shalom" was a common Jewish greeting. It meant more than the absence of conflict; it expressed a desire that the one "greeted will have all the righteousness and goodness

God can give. The deepest meaning of the term is 'God's highest good to you.'"[41] In addition, it must be noticed that Christ doesn't say blessed are those who "love peace," but blessed are "the peacemakers." Everybody loves the concept of peace, but very few are willing to be active in creating it. It is impossible to have peace without God's righteousness. Peace without righteousness is just a truce with sin. The pursuit of true peace often results in trouble. Christ said, "I didn't come to bring peace, but to bring a sword" (Matt 10:34, paraphrase). Christ, the Prince of Peace (Is 9:6), realized that to have true peace, there must, at times, be conflict. Christ died to reconcile God and people (Rom 5:1), and people with one another (Eph 2:14-18). Often a peacemaker is somebody who comes between two warring parties and takes the blows from each side in order to create peace.

What does it look like practically to be a peacemaker?

1. Peacemakers seek to reconcile people with God.

    Second Corinthians 5:18-21 says:

    And all these things are from God who reconciled us to himself through Christ, and who has given us the ministry of reconciliation. In other words, in Christ God was reconciling the world to himself, not counting people's trespasses against them, and he has given us the message of reconciliation. Therefore we are ambassadors for Christ, as though God were making His plea through us. We plead with you on Christ's behalf, "Be reconciled to God!" God made the one who did not know sin to be sin for us, so that in him we would become the righteousness of God.

    God is a holy God and therefore cannot have a relationship with sinful people. Therefore, all people are under the wrath of God because of our sins. The Gospel message is the truth that Christ bore God's wrath on the cross for our sins, so we can have a right relationship with God. Romans 5:1 says, "Therefore, since we have been declared righteous by faith, we have peace with God through our Lord Jesus Christ." Peacemakers are those who devote their lives to sharing this message. Because they have experienced it, they share it with others—hoping to reconcile people with God.

Are you sharing the Gospel message? This is what peacemakers do.

2. Peacemakers seek to reconcile people.

This starts with us and our relationship with others. Matthew 5:23-24 says that if we go to the altar to offer a gift and realize that somebody has something against us, we should leave the gift, reconcile with the person, and then offer the gift to God. Romans 12:18 says, "If possible, so far as it depends on you, live peaceably with all people." We forgive those who have sinned against us. We bless and don't curse them. We humble ourselves and ask for forgiveness from those we sinned against. Because we've been reconciled with God, we seek to reconcile with others.

Not only do we seek to reconcile with others, but we seek to help others reconcile. In Philippians 4:2-3, Paul says,

> I appeal to Euodia and to Syntyche to agree in the Lord. Yes, I say also to you, true companion, help them. They have struggled together in the gospel ministry along with me and Clement and my other coworkers, whose names are in the book of life.

Paul understood that division tends to spread, as people take sides. It opens the door for Satan (Eph 4:26-27) and removes the blessing of God from a community (Ps 133). Therefore, though Paul was away in prison, he urged two women in Philippi to reconcile. He also petitioned a member of the church to help them. In 1 Corinthians 6:1-11, when believers were suing one another before unbelievers, Paul called for the church to appoint wise men in the congregation to judge the dispute. He also counseled them to accept being wronged (even as Christ taught us to turn the other cheek) for the sake of unity. Satan is the divider, but Christ is the reconciler. Therefore, Christians aid Christ in this reconciliation mission. This means listening to others, exposing points of commonality, bringing God's Word to bear upon the situation, and leading people towards a resolution.

3. Peacemakers confront sin in hopes of fostering righteousness.

This again starts with the peacemaker's own life. In Matthew 7:3-5, Christ taught that if we are going to take the speck out of our neighbor's eye, we must first take the log out of our own eye. Christ also said that if our eye offends us, we should pluck it out, and if our hand offends us, we should cut it off (Matt 5:29-30). In other words, believers should be ruthless in seeking to get rid of personal sin. As we conquer wrong thoughts and actions in our own life, we are more effective in leading others out of sin.

In Matthew 18:15-17, Christ lays out the process for confronting sin in others. He said:

> "If your brother sins, go and show him his fault when the two of you are alone. If he listens to you, you have regained your brother. But if he does not listen, take one or two others with you, so that at the testimony of two or three witnesses every matter may be established. If he refuses to listen to them, tell it to the church. If he refuses to listen to the church, treat him like a Gentile or a tax collector.

If a brother is in sin, we should confront him one-on-one. Most fail at this first point. Some fail because their contention is not a sin issue at all—it is a preference or wisdom issue. We shouldn't treat sin the same as a preference or wisdom issue. Christ flipped tables and pulled out a whip over sin (John 2). He also went to the cross over it. Sadly, many do this over non-sin issues—dividing relationships, ministries, and work places. When in a potential conflict, one must ask, "Is this a sin or non-sin issue?" This type of deliberation will end many conflicts before they start.

Others fail at Christ's direction by sharing the sin with others first—causing more conflict. Proverbs 16:28 says a whisperer separates friends. Or, they fail by not confronting the person at all. We say to ourselves, "This has nothing to do with me," "It is his choice," and so on. However, sin always affects more than just the person sinning. It dishonors God, and it hurts others, even if only by modeling sin—leading to its spread. Paul said a little leaven leavens the whole lump (1 Cor 5:6). If sin isn't confronted in the body of Christ, it will spread to others. Therefore, the peacemaker, in obedience to God, confronts sin. He or she speaks the truth in love (Eph 4:15). If the person in sin doesn't respond, he brings one or two others to petition the person to repent. If this doesn't work, he brings it before the church. And if the person still doesn't respond, the church disciplines the believer. As mentioned, if this process of confronting sin is not happening in a church, sin infects, spreads, and ultimately kills. It pushes people away from God and his Church.

This is a difficult ministry, but God says that he blesses the peacemaker. Christ confronted the Pharisees—the spiritual leaders who were misleading Israel. Christ confronted those who were being dishonest at the temple. He ultimately confronted all sin at the cross, as he bore the penalty for everyone's sins so they could be reconciled to God.

Are you willing to confront sin—both yours and others? If so, you must desire God's blessing more than the blessing of others.

Application Question: What makes this ministry so difficult? Why do so many choose to not participate in it? In what ways have you had to participate in peacemaking in the past? What were the results? Is there a specific situation that you feel God calling you to intervene and help bring peace?

Growth as a Peacemaker

Application Question: How can we grow as peacemakers?

1. To grow as peacemakers, we must continually get rid of sin in our own lives.

The more we conquer sin in our lives, the more effective we will be at helping others conquer it. People will more likely listen to us if we're walking right with God than if we're not. Also, we'll be more successful at counseling others on how to be set free, if we're experiencing victory ourselves. Therefore, we must continually confess and repent of sin to be effective at this ministry.

2. To grow as peacemakers, we must be painfully honest.

Jeremiah said this about the false prophets: "They dress the wound of my people as though it were not serious. 'Peace, peace,' they say, when there is no peace" (6:14 NIV). Where false prophets ignore the problem or don't recognize the seriousness of it, peacemakers call sin, sin, and rebellion, rebellion. We must recognize sin in our own life and others. First John 1:9 says, "If we confess our sins, he is faithful and just to forgive us our sins and to cleanse us from all unrighteousness." The Greek word for "confess" means to "say the same thing." We must see our sin, and that of others, the same way God does. It put Christ on the cross; it divides us from God and others. If we are going to grow as peacemakers, we must be brutally honest about sin both individually and corporately.

3. To grow as peacemakers, we must be willing to risk pain.

Any time we confront sin—seeking to restore people to God and others—we risk being misunderstood, hated, and even persecuted. Such is the lot of peacemakers. As mentioned, it is no surprise that the next beatitude is, "Blessed are those who are persecuted for righteousness." If we are going to be peacemakers, we must be willing to risk pain. Proverbs 27:6 says, "Faithful are the wounds of a friend"—true friends are willing to hurt each other, in love, in order to heal each other.

4. To grow as peacemakers, we must develop healthy communication skills.

- Healthy communication includes being a good listener. James 1:19 says, "Understand this, my dear brothers and sisters! Let every person be quick to listen, slow to speak, slow to anger." Note that he says we should be "quick to listen." Literally, we must hurry up to listen. Typically, we only hurry up to speak. This leads to misunderstanding, as we often lack all the facts. As believers, we must listen to (1) what a person is saying, (2) and what a person is not saying. This includes asking clarifying questions to discern what's really going on and the root of the issues. (3) We also must listen to the Holy Spirit. We should shoot arrow prayers up to God when engaging in a potentially explosive conversation. That's what Nehemiah did, while talking with the King of Persia about restoring the walls of Jerusalem (Neh 2:4). This conversation could have led to his execution; therefore, he bathed it with prayer.

- Healthy communication includes choosing our words and tone carefully. Proverbs 17:27 says, "The truly wise person restrains his words, and the one who stays calm is discerning." To restrain one's words means to weigh them and consider their potential effect, instead of simply speaking without much deliberation. We should ask ourselves, "Could this offend or hurt somebody?" "Is this the best way to say this?" A fool just says what's on his heart—not considering how others might respond (Prov 29:11). In addition, thought must be given to the tone of our words. Proverbs 15:1 says, "A gentle response turns away wrath, but a harsh word stirs up wrath." It has been said that communication is seventy percent nonverbal including body language and tone.

- Healthy communication includes controlling our anger. James 1:20 says, "For human anger does not accomplish God's righteousness." Proverbs 15:18 says, "A quick-tempered person stirs up dissension, but one who is slow to anger calms a quarrel."

5. To grow as peacemakers, we must return good for evil.

Since the peacemaker is often misunderstood, criticized, and even persecuted, he must make peace by sowing seeds of peace. Romans 12:18-20 says,

> If possible, so far as it depends on you, live peaceably with all people. Do not avenge yourselves, dear friends, but give place to God's wrath, for it is written, "Vengeance is mine, I will repay," says the Lord. Rather, if your enemy is hungry, feed him; if he is thirsty, give him a drink; for in doing this you will be heaping burning coals on his head. Do not be overcome by evil, but overcome evil with good.

As we sow peace, Lord willing, it will create righteousness. James 3:18 (NIV) says, "Peacemakers who sow in peace reap a harvest of righteousness." Are you returning good for evil?

6. To grow as peacemakers, we must develop perseverance.

Often sin takes a long time to root out. Our evangelism, prayers, and conflict resolution will often not immediately produce positive fruit. However, Galatians 6:9 encourages us, "So we must not grow weary in doing good, for in due time we will reap, if we do not give up."

Don't give up. There is a proper time for a harvest, and that time is within God's sovereign plan. He will produce fruit, if we don't give up.

7. To grow as peacemakers, we must trust God.

We cannot actually create peace; only God can. We must sow the right seeds and trust God. Second Timothy 2:24-25 (NIV) says,

> And the Lord's servant must not be quarrelsome but must be kind to everyone, able to teach, not resentful. Opponents must be gently instructed, in the hope that God will grant them repentance leading them to a knowledge of the truth

The Lord's servant doesn't quarrel because his hope is in God. Only God can change hearts. We plant seeds and water them, but God makes it grow (1 Cor 3:6). We must remember this.

In addition, part of trusting in God is being faithful in prayer. We should fight our battles in prayer before we fight them in person. We should pray for blindness to be removed from people's eyes, Satan to be bound, right words to say, and God to bring truth and righteousness.

Are you growing as a peacemaker?

Application Question: Which aspect of growing as a peacemaker do you feel most called to develop? Are there specific skills that you feel stronger at? Which ones? What are some other ways to grow or become more efficient at peacemaking?

Sons of God

Interpretation Question: What does it mean to be called sons of God?

In this context, the phrase "children of God" is better translated "sons of God"[42] (cf. the ESV and NASB versions), since, in Jewish thought, the term 'son' bears the meaning "partaker of the character of."[43] For example, when Christ sent the disciples on missions, he told them to look for a house with a "son of peace." "Son of peace" simply means a peaceful person (Lk 10:6 KJV). When Barnabas was called a "son of encouragement," it meant he was an encouraging person (Acts 4:36). Therefore, to be called a "son of God" refers to someone who is Godlike—demonstrating God's character. In the same way that Christ came to earth to reconcile people with God and people with one another, "sons of God" participate in the same ministry.[44]

The verb "shall be called" is a continuous future passive. It means that believers will not call themselves sons of God. Others will do so, and this will happen throughout eternity.[45]

The reward of peacemakers reminds us that those who continually participate in God-like peace-making are truly born again—truly children of God. If we don't participate, then we may not be. Kent Hughes puts it this way:

> If we are not peacemakers but troublemakers, there is high probability that we are not true children of God, regardless of how prominently we wear our evangelicalism. Peacemakers are sometimes troublemakers for the sake of peace, but not troublemakers who spread rumors and gossip about others. If you are constantly fomenting discontent, if you find joy in the report of trouble and scandal, if you are omnicritical, always fault-finding, if you are unwilling to be involved in peacemaking, if you are mean—if these negative qualities characterize your life, you are probably not a true Christian (cf. 1 Corinthians 6:9–11; Galatians 5:19–21 on the fate of those involved in slander, hatred, discord, dissension, and factions).[46]

MacArthur adds:

Peacemaking is a hallmark of God's children. A person who is not a peacemaker either is not a Christian or is a disobedient Christian. The person who is continually disruptive, divisive, and quarrelsome has good reason to doubt his relationship to God altogether. God's sons-that is, all of His children, both male and female-are peacemakers. Only God determines who His children are, and He has determined that they are the humble, the penitent over sin, the gentle, the seekers of righteousness, the merciful, the pure in heart, and the peacemakers.[47]

Are you a peacemaker? If so, God calls you a son or daughter of God—a partaker in his character—and others will know you by this designation throughout eternity.

Application Question: Are there any prominent peacemakers—sons or daughters of God—who come to your mind when you think of this beatitude? How do you feel called to model them?

Conclusion

"Blessed are the peacemakers for they shall be called sons of God." Christ, the Son of God, was called the Prince of Peace. He brought peace between God and people, and people with others. He has committed this same ministry—the ministry of reconciliation—to us. It is a difficult ministry. Many want peace at all costs, but sons and daughters of God will not forsake righteousness or truth to have peace. That is just a truce with sin—something God will never do. There is often a cost for peace, and peacemakers are often the ones who pay it. Christ bore a cross and so must his disciples. Are you willing to pay the cost for peace? Lord, help us to be faithful peacemakers who reap a harvest of righteousness.

Blessed Are the Persecuted

> "Blessed are those who are persecuted for righteousness, for the kingdom of heaven belongs to them. Blessed are you when people insult you and persecute you and say all kinds of evil things about you falsely on account of me. Rejoice and be glad because your reward is great in heaven, for they persecuted the prophets before you in the same way.
> Matthew 5:10-12 (NET)

The first seven Beatitudes lead naturally into the eighth. The more we demonstrate the characteristics of the kingdom in our lives, the more we will be persecuted by the world. Persecution is the gold stamp on the believer's life. The last beatitude is the only one with a double blessing. Christ says, "Blessed are those who are persecuted for righteousness" (v.10) and "Blessed are you when people insult you" (v.11). It is these people and these alone who are part of the kingdom of heaven.

We must consider this beatitude well, as it will sustain us in dark times. When Charles Spurgeon was severely depressed over the criticism he received in his ministry, his wife printed all eight beatitudes on a large sheet of paper and tacked it on the ceiling above his bed. She wanted him to remember, first thing in the morning and last at night, that the righteous will be persecuted. There are no exceptions, and we must remember this as well.[48]

In Matthew 24:9, Christ taught that in the end times believers will be hated by all nations because of him. Persecution will only continue to grow as this world gets further away from God. As this world becomes darker, the light in believers will become even more offensive. Already, more Christians have died for the faith in the last century, than the other centuries combined. How can we remain faithful in suffering?

In this study, we will consider the persecution believers experience because of righteousness, the joy to be found in it, and its reward.

Big Question: What is the meaning of the eighth beatitude and what are some applications from it?

Persecuted

Interpretation Question: What does it mean to be persecuted?

The word "persecuted" means to "pursue" or "chase." It can also be translated "harass."[49] In verse 11, Christ says, "Blessed are you 'when' people insult you". "When" can also be translated "whenever." This means that believers will not always be persecuted. They will experience times of peace and possibly times of popularity. Even Christ was not persecuted all the time.[50]

"Persecuted" is a passive perfect participle and could thus be translated "allow themselves to be persecuted."[51] What is shocking about these believers is that they are willing to undergo persecution in order to pursue righteousness, preach truth, and to honor God. They are willing to bear their cross for Christ's sake (cf. Lk 14:27).

Observation Question: What are the three types of persecution Christ lists that believers will at times experience?

1. "Insult" literally means to "to cast in one's teeth."[52] This probably refers to people negatively talking about believers to their faces.
2. "Persecute," in the context of verse 11, probably refers to physical abuse, such as imprisonment.
3. "Falsely say all kinds of evil against you" may refer to being talked about behind their backs.

There will be times and seasons when Christians experience each of these.

Interpretation Question: Why will believers be persecuted?

Christ gave two reasons: "for righteousness" in verse 10 and "on account of me" in verse 11. These two statements are clearly parallel—referring to the same thing. As with Abel, Cain killed him not because of something he did wrong but because of something he did right. Abel offered an acceptable sacrifice to God which enraged Cain. Obviously, this also happened to Christ. John 3:19-20 comments on the world's response to Christ:

> Now this is the basis for judging: that the light has come into the world and people loved the darkness rather than the light, because their deeds were evil. For everyone who does evil deeds hates the light and does not come to the light, so that their deeds will not be exposed.

When people are living in sin, they naturally will hate those living in righteousness. To be the honest person in a class room where everybody is cheating (and to possibly report or speak out against those who are cheating) will provoke persecution. To work at a business, where others regularly gossip, talk negatively about the leadership, get drunk after work, practice dishonesty, etc., and be the one to decline to participate will again stir up resentment. It may lead to being harassed, passed over for promotion, or even fired. With Daniel, his co-workers got him tossed into the lion's den (Dan 6). You may not face lions, but your persecution will increase as you, like Christ, expose sin and call for righteousness. Therefore, harassment, ostracism, and persecution are the lot of faithful believers.

Persecution for righteousness also happens as a result of spiritual warfare. In Job 1, when God drew attention to Job's righteousness, it led Satan to accuse Job and seek permission to afflict him. Job lost his job, family, and eventually his health, and it was all rooted in the spiritual realm; he was attacked because of his righteousness. This commonly happens to believers, especially when they are on fire for God. Satan will afflict them because of their righteousness in order to deter them from living for God. To do this, he not only uses demons but also the world.

Interpretation Question: How was persecution experienced in the early church?

Persecution was experienced in at least three ways:

1. Persecution often manifested in one's family life.

Typically, a child might become saved but the parents and siblings would not. A wife would accept Christ while the husband refused. As result, some believers were shunned, beaten, disowned, and possibly killed over their faith.

2. Persecution often manifested in one's social life.

Social gatherings and celebrations commonly happened at temples. People would bring meat to be sacrificed; a portion was burned for the gods and another portion was given to the priests, but the majority went to those who sacrificed. They would celebrate by eating and drinking at the temples in honor of the gods. The typical invitation would say something like: "I invite you to dine at the table of our Lord Serapis"[53] (or the name of some other god). This excluded Christians from those gatherings. How could they participate in a celebration meant to honor pagan gods? This even affected ordinary dinners at a neighbors' house. Typically, before eating dinner, pagans would offer food and drink to their idols—similar to how Christians asks for the Lord's blessing over their meals. How could a Christian participate with a clear conscience? Again, this led to separation, hatred, and ostracism.

3. Persecution often manifested in one's work life.

Much of the ancient work life was also centered around worshiping the gods. A blacksmith might be offered a contract to make idols, or a mason to work on temples. This again would affect the conscience of Christians. In addition, cheating, cutting corners, and bribery was common in the work force. To refuse could lead to not only being hated but also losing employment. This was the lot of early Christians.

Tertullian, a second-century Christian leader, was approached by a man who said, "I have come to Christ, but I don't know what to do. I have a job that I don't think is consistent with what Scripture teaches. What can I do? I must live." Tertullian replied, "Must you?" For Tertullian, there was only one option: Obey and honor Christ—survival was secondary.[54]

Heightened Persecution

At times, this persecution grew to startling heights. Under Nero, Christians were burned as torches to light up his garden. Meat was tied to Christians' bodies, and they were given to the dogs to be torn apart in the amphitheater. By the end of the first century, the Roman emperors became deified. As the empire expanded, it became the primary way Romans tried to keep unity between all the nations under their rule. People could worship other gods and speak different languages, but they had to declare that Caesar was Lord. It was compulsory to give a verbal oath of this once a year. When completed, they would receive a verifying certificate called a libellus. After this public proclamation, people could continue to freely worship other gods. However, this was something faithful Christians refused to do, and therefore were considered traitors. Because of their refusal, they suffered the confiscation of property, loss of work, imprisonment, and often death.[55]

Certainly, Christians could avoid persecution by compromising their faith—declaring that Caesar was Lord, honoring the gods at the temples and people's homes, and by not speaking out against sinful practices—and indeed, some did. However, Christ taught that in order to be his disciples, we must hate father, mother, and other family members. We must be willing to take up our cross (Lk 14:26-27). A "disciple" who is unwilling to bear his cross is no disciple at all, and according to this final beatitude, he is not part of God's kingdom. In fact, Christ taught that those who denied him before others, he would also deny before the Father (Matt 10:33). In Luke 6:26, he declared, "Woe to you when all people speak well of you, for their ancestors did the same things to the false prophets." Bearing the character of the Beatitudes always leads to bearing the persecution of the final beatitude. It won't always be extreme in nature, such as imprisonment or burning; often it will be subtle—like being considered strange, weird, or archaic (cf. 1 Pet 3:16, 4:4)—but it will be there if we are truly part of the kingdom.

Are you willing to take up your cross to follow Christ?

Application Question: In what ways do you see persecution towards Christians growing in the world today? How have you experienced persecution for righteousness? How should a Christian respond if he or she lacks some form of persecution for righteousness?

Rejoicing in Persecution

Observation Question: How should believers respond to this persecution?

Believers are not called to retaliate or return evil for evil. We are not called to sulk in self-pity over our persecution. In verse 12, Christ calls believers to "Rejoice and be glad." "Be glad" can literally be translated, "Leap for joy!" And this is what has happened throughout biblical history. In Acts 5:41, the apostles, after being flogged by the Sanhedrin, left rejoicing because they had been counted worthy to suffer for the name. In Acts 16:25, while in prison, Paul and Silas were praying and singing hymns. They rejoiced in the midst of their suffering.

Surprisingly, joy in suffering is not an uncommon experience for those being persecuted for the faith. Kent Hughes shares two powerful testimonies:

> Samuel Rutherford, the saintly Scottish pastor, wrote from his prison sty, "I never knew by my nine years of preaching so much of Christ's love, as He taught me in Aberdeen by six months imprisonment." "Christ's cross," he also said, "is such a burden as sails are to a ship or wings to a bird."
>
> And in our own time a Romanian pastor describes how he was imprisoned and tortured mercilessly and yet experienced joy. Locked in solitary confinement, he had been summoned by his captors, who cut chunks of flesh from his body, and was then returned to his cell, where he was starved. Yet in the midst of this sadism, there were times when the joy of Christ so overcame him that he would pull himself up and shuffle about the cell in holy dance. So remarkable was his joy that on his release from prison and his return to his home, he chose to fast the first day in memorial to the joy he had known in prison.[56]

Interpretation Question: How is joy possible in the midst of great suffering for Christ?

1. Joy in suffering for Christ is a Divine bestowal.

This beatitude, as with the others, begins with "Blessed," which can be translated "Happy." When believers are willing to accept persecution for the sake of righteousness, God gives them a divine bestowal of joy. This has been the experience of believers throughout history. Like Stephen being "full of the Holy Spirit" as he saw Christ before being stoned in Act 7:55, many experience intimacy with God while suffering for the faith—resulting in great joy.

2. Joy in suffering for Christ is a discipline.

When Christ calls for us to "Rejoice and be glad," these verbs are imperatives in the Greek. Therefore, they are not mere suggestions, but holy commands from our Lord. We must, as an act of obedience, choose to rejoice and leap for joy when criticized and thought strange for Christ. We do this in the same way that we seek to give thanks in everything, as this is God's will for us in Christ Jesus (1 Thess 5:18).

3. Joy in suffering for Christ is a result of redeemed thinking.

Observation Question: What type of thinking leads to joy in the midst of suffering for righteousness, as demonstrated in Matthew 5:10-12?

(1) We must remember that suffering for righteousness, as with the rest of the Beatitudes, is a proof of our salvation. Christ says this about those persecuted for righteousness, "for the kingdom of heaven belongs to them." "Them" is emphatic in the Greek—meaning "them alone." Thus, to be without some form of persecution may prove we are not truly saved. (2) We must remember that suffering for righteousness will be greatly rewarded in heaven. James 1:12 says, "Happy is the one who endures testing, because when he has proven to be genuine, he will receive the crown of life that God promised to those who love him." (3) We must remember that suffering for righteousness puts us in the company of the prophets. Elijah was hunted by Ahab and Jezebel. Jeremiah was imprisoned and tradition says stoned to death. Similarly, Isaiah was sawed in half. John the Baptist was beheaded. Jesus was crucified. Stephen was stoned. Ten of the eleven disciples (excluding the betrayer, Judas) were martyred. John, the eleventh, was exiled to the Island of Patmos by the Emperor Domitian. As we rightly consider suffering for righteousness, it should cause us to be glad—literally leap for joy! Paul taught that just as belief in Christ is a gift of God so is suffering for him. Philippians 1:29 says, "For it has been granted

to you not only to believe in Christ but also to suffer for him." Suffering for the faith is a gift from God, and therefore we should rejoice in it.

Interpretation Question: What are some other reasons that Scripture says we should rejoice in suffering?

(4) Scripture also teaches that we can rejoice because suffering produces perseverance in us, character, and hope in God (Rom 5:3-4). (5) We can rejoice in suffering because it makes us weak, and therefore, more able to display God's power. God told Paul that his power was made perfect in weakness (2 Cor 12:7-8)—leading Paul to boast in his weaknesses and infirmities (v. 9-10). (6) We can rejoice in suffering because in the midst of it, we experience God's comfort and therefore are equipped to offer comfort to others who suffer. Second Corinthians 1:3-4 says,

> Blessed is the God and Father of our Lord Jesus Christ, the Father of mercies and God of all comfort, who comforts us in all our troubles so that we may be able to comfort those experiencing any trouble with the comfort with which we ourselves are comforted by God.

As we rightly think on suffering for Christ and sufferings in general, we realize that though suffering is a cross to bear, it is also a crown to wear. The benefits are exceedingly great—so much so that biblically-minded Christians can truly leap for joy in them. God is working in believers for his good—making them into the image of Christ to the glory of God (Rom 8:28-29). Thank you, Lord, for your faithfulness in using the cross for the good! Amen!

Application Question: What are your thoughts about the possibility of experiencing joy in the midst of suffering for Christ? Why is this possible? How have you experienced joy in the midst of trials in general?

Conclusion

Paul told his protégé, Timothy, that "Now in fact all who want to live godly lives in Christ Jesus will be persecuted" (2 Tim 3:12). This is an inescapable fact. And, as this world becomes darker, the light that shines from believers will become even more offensive—leading every nation to hate Christians (Matt 24:9). Already, more Christians have died in the last century for the faith, than the other centuries combined.

However, let us remember that afflictions we experience in this life are light in comparison to the weight of glory and reward we will experience in heaven (2 Cor 4:17). We should consider it a gift to experience what our Lord suffered on this earth (cf. Phil 1:29). It means we are looking more like him. In addition, we also must remember when it is time to suffer for Christ's name, grace will be available. The grace that saved us and the grace that sanctifies us will be available so we can suffer in a way that glorifies Christ (cf. Phil 1:19-20). Thank you, Lord!

Appendix 1

Study Group Tips

Leading a small group using the Bible Teacher's Guide can be done in various ways. One format for leading a small group is the "study group" model, where each member prepares and shares in the teaching. This appendix will cover tips for facilitating a weekly study group.

1. Each week the members of the study group will read through a select chapter of the guide, answer the reflection questions (see Appendix 2), and come prepared to share in the group.

2. Prior to each meeting, a different member can be selected to lead the group and share Question 1 of the reflection questions, which is to give a short summary of the chapter read. This section of the gathering could last from five to fifteen minutes. This way, each member can develop their gift of teaching. It also will make them study harder during the week. Or, each week the same person could share the summary.

3. After the summary has been given, the leader for that week will facilitate discussions through the rest of the reflection questions and also ask select review questions from the chapter.

4. After discussion, the group will share prayer requests and pray for one another.

The strength of the study group is the fact that the members will be required to prepare their responses before the meeting, which will allow for easier discussion. In addition, each member will be given the opportunity to teach, which will further equip their ministry skills. The study group model has distinct advantages.

Appendix 2

Reflection Questions

Writing is one of the best ways to learn. In class, we take notes and write papers, and all these methods are used to help us learn and retain the material. The same is true with the Word of God. Obviously, all the authors of Scripture were writers. This helped them better learn the Scriptures and also enabled them to more effectively teach it. In studying God's Word with the Bible Teacher's Guide, take time to write so you can similarly grow both in your learning and teaching.

1. How would you summarize the main points of the text/chapter? Write a brief summary.

2. What stood out to you most in the reading? Did any of the contents trigger any memories or experiences? If so, please share them.

3. What follow-up questions did you have about the reading? What parts did you not fully agree with?

4. What applications did you take from the reading, and how do you plan to implement them into your life?

5. Write several commitment statements: As a result of my time studying God's Word, I will . . .

6. What are some practical ways to pray as a result of studying the text? Spend some time ministering to the Lord through prayer.

Appendix 3

Walking the Romans Road

How can a person be saved? From what is he saved? How can someone have eternal life? Scripture teaches that after death each person will spend eternity either in heaven or hell. How can a person go to heaven?

Paul said this to Timothy:

> You, however, must continue in the things you have learned and are confident about. You know who taught you and how from infancy you have known the holy writings, which are able to give you wisdom for salvation through faith in Christ Jesus.
> 2 Timothy 3:14-15

One of the reasons God gave us Scripture is to make us wise for salvation. This means that without it nobody can know how to be saved.

Well then, how can a people be saved and what are they being saved from? A common method of sharing the good news of salvation is through the Romans Road. One of the great themes, not only of the Bible, but specifically of the book of Romans is salvation. In Romans, the author, Paul, clearly details the steps we must take in order to be saved.

How can we be saved? What steps must we take?

Step One: We Must Accept that We Are Sinners

Romans 3:23 says, "For all have sinned and fall short of the glory of God." What does it mean to sin? The word sin means "to miss the mark." The mark we missed is looking like God. When God created mankind in the Genesis narrative, he created man in the "image of God" (1:27). The "image of God" means many things, but probably, most importantly it means we were made to be holy just as he is holy. Man was made moral. We were meant to reflect God's holiness in every way: the way we think, the way we talk, and the way we act. And any time we miss the mark in these areas, we commit sin.

Furthermore, we do not only sin when we commit a sinful act such as: lying, stealing, or cheating. Again, we sin anytime we have a wrong heart motive. The greatest commandments in Scripture are to "Love the Lord your God with all your heart and to love your neighbor as yourself" (Matt 22:36-40, paraphrase). Whenever we don't love God supremely and love others as ourselves, we sin and fall short of the glory of God. For this reason, man is always in a state of sinning. Sadly, even if our actions are good, our heart is bad. I have never loved God with my whole heart, mind, and soul and neither has anybody else. Therefore, we have all sinned and fall short of the glory of God (Rom 3:23). We have all missed the mark of God's holiness and we must accept this.

What's the next step?

Step Two: We Must Understand We Are Under the Judgment of God

Why are we under the judgment of God? It is because of our sins. Scripture teaches God is not only a loving God, but he is a just God. And his justice requires judgment for each of our sins. Romans 6:23 says, "For the payoff of sin is death."

A wage is something we earn. Every time we sin, we earn the wage of death. What is death? Death really means separation. In physical death, the body is separated from the spirit, but in spiritual death, man is separated from God. Man currently lives in a state of spiritual death (cf. Eph 2:1-3). We do not love God, obey him, or know him as we should. Therefore, man is in a state of death.

Moreover, one day at our physical death, if we have not been saved, we will spend eternity separated from God in a very real hell. In hell, we will pay the wage for each of our sins. Therefore, in hell people will experience various degrees of punishment (cf. Lk 12:47-48). This places man in a very dangerous predicament—unholy and therefore under the judgment of God.

How should we respond to this? This leads us to our third step.

Step Three: We Must Recognize God Has Invited All to Accept His Free Gift of Salvation

Romans 6:23 does not stop at the wages of sin being death. It says, "For the payoff of sin is death, but the gift of God is eternal life in Christ Jesus our Lord." Because God loved everybody on the earth, he offered the free gift of eternal life, which anyone can receive through Jesus Christ.

Because it is a gift, it cannot be earned. We cannot work for it. Ephesians 2:8-9 says, "For by grace you are saved through faith, and this is not from yourselves, it is the gift of God; it is not from works, so that no one can boast."

Going to church, being baptized, giving to the poor, or doing any other righteous work does not save. Salvation is a gift that must be received from God. It is a gift that has been prepared by his effort alone.

How do we receive this free gift?

Step Four: We Must Believe Jesus Christ Died for Our Sins and Rose from the Dead

If we are going to receive this free gift, we must believe in God's Son, Jesus Christ. Because God loved us, cared for us, and didn't want us to be separated from him eternally, he sent his Son to die for our sins. Romans 5:8 says, "But God demonstrates his own love for us, in that while we were still sinners, Christ died for us."

Similarly, John 3:16 says, "For this is the way God loved the world: He gave his one and only Son, so that everyone who believes in him will not perish but have eternal life." God so loved us that he gave his only Son for our sins.

Jesus Christ was a real, historical person who lived 2,000 years ago. He was born of a virgin. He lived a perfect life. He was put to death by the Romans and the Jews. And he rose again on the third day. In his death, he took our sins and God's wrath for them and gave us his perfect righteousness so we could be accepted by God. Second Corinthians 5:21 says, "God made the one who did not know sin to be sin for us, so that in him we would become the righteousness of God." God did all this so we could be saved from his wrath.

Christ's death satisfied the just anger of God over our sins. When God saw Jesus on the cross, he saw us and our sins and therefore judged Jesus. And now, when God sees those who are saved, he sees his righteous Son and accepts us. In salvation, we have become the righteousness of God.

If we are going to be saved, if we are going to receive this free gift of salvation, we must believe in Christ's death, burial, and resurrection for our sins (cf. 1 Cor 15:3-5, Rom 10:9-10). Do you believe?

Step Five: We Must Confess Christ as Lord of Our Lives

Romans 10:9-10 says,

> Because if you confess with your mouth that Jesus is Lord and believe in your heart that God raised him from the dead, you will be saved. For with the heart one believes and thus has righteousness and with the mouth one confesses and thus has salvation.

Not only must we believe, but we must confess Christ as Lord of our lives. It is one thing to believe in Christ but another to follow Christ. Simple belief does not save. Christ must be our Lord.

James said this: "...Even the demons believe that – and tremble with fear" (James 2:19), but the demons are not saved—Christ is not their Lord.

Another aspect of making Christ Lord is repentance. Repentance really means a change of mind that leads to a change of direction. Before we met Christ, we were living our own life and following our own sinful desires. But when we get saved, our mind and direction change. We start to follow Christ as Lord.

How do we make this commitment to the lordship of Christ so we can be saved? Paul said we must confess with our mouth "Jesus is Lord" as we believe in him. Romans 10:13 says, "For everyone who calls on the name of the Lord will be saved."

If you admit that you are a sinner and understand you are under God's wrath because of them; if you believe Jesus Christ is the Son of God, that he died on the cross for your sins, and rose from the dead for your salvation; if you are ready to turn from your sin and cling to Christ as Lord, you can be saved.

If this is your heart, then you can pray this prayer and commit to following Christ as your Lord.

> *Dear heavenly Father, I confess I am a sinner and have fallen short of your glory, what you made me for. I believe Jesus Christ died on the cross to pay the penalty for my sins and rose from the dead so I can have eternal life. I am turning away from my sin and accepting you as my Lord and Savior. Come into my life and change me. Thank you for your gift of salvation.*

Scripture teaches that if you truly accepted Christ as your Lord, then you are a new creation. Second Corinthians 5:17 says, "So then, if anyone is in Christ, he is a new creation; what is old has passed away – look, what is new has come!" God has forgiven your sins (1 John 1:9), he has given you his Holy Spirit (Rom 8:15), and he is going to disciple you and make you into the image of his Son (cf. Rom 8:29). He will never leave you nor forsake you (Heb 13:5), and he will complete the work he has begun in your life (Phil

1:6). In heaven, angels and saints are rejoicing because of your commitment to Christ (Lk 15:7).

Praise God for his great salvation! May God keep you in his hand, empower you through the Holy Spirit, train you through mature believers, and use you to build his kingdom! "He who calls you is trustworthy, and he will in fact do this" (1 Thess 5:24). God bless you!

Coming Soon

Praise the Lord for your interest in studying and teaching God's Word. If God has blessed you through the BTG series, please partner with us in petitioning God to greatly use this series to encourage and build his Church. Also, please consider leaving an Amazon review and signing up for free book promotions. By doing this, you help spread the "Word." Thanks for your partnership in the gospel from the first day until now (Phil 1:4-5).

Available:
First Peter
Theology Proper
Building Foundations for a Godly Marriage
Colossians
God's Battle Plan for Purity
Nehemiah
Philippians
The Perfections of God
The Armor of God
Ephesians
Abraham
Finding a Godly Mate
1 Timothy
The Beatitudes
Equipping Small Group Leaders
2 Timothy
Jacob

Coming Soon:
The Sermon on the Mount

About the Author

Greg Brown received his MA in religion and MA in teaching from Trinity International University, a MRE from Liberty University, and a PhD in theology from Louisiana Baptist University. He has served over fourteen years in pastoral ministry and currently serves as chaplain and professor at Handong Global University, teaching pastor at Handong International Congregation, and as a Navy Reserve chaplain.

Greg married his lovely wife, Tara Jayne, in 2006, and they have one daughter, Saiyah Grace. He enjoys going on dates with his wife, playing with his daughter, reading, writing, studying in coffee shops, working out, and following the NBA and UFC. His pursuit in life, simply stated, is "to know God and to be found faithful by Him."

To connect with Greg, please follow at
http://www.pgregbrown.com.

Notes

[1] Hughes, R. K. (2001). *The sermon on the mount: the message of the kingdom* (p. 16). Wheaton, IL: Crossway Books.
[2] Guzik, D. (2013). *Matthew* (Mt 5:2). Santa Barbara, CA: David Guzik.
[3] Hughes, R. K. (2001). *The sermon on the mount: the message of the kingdom* (pp. 16–17). Wheaton, IL: Crossway Books.
[4] Wiersbe, W. W. (1996). *The Bible exposition commentary* (Vol. 1, p. 21). Wheaton, IL: Victor Books.
[5] Carson, D. A. (1999). *Jesus' Sermon on the Mount and His Confrontation with the World: An Exposition of Matthew 5–10* (p. 17). Grand Rapids, MI: Baker Academic.
[6] Hughes, R. K. (2001). *The sermon on the mount: the message of the kingdom* (p. 17). Wheaton, IL: Crossway Books.
[7] Guzik, D. (2013). *Matthew* (Mt 5:3–12). Santa Barbara, CA: David Guzik.
[8] MacArthur, J. F., Jr. (1985). *Matthew* (pp. 140–142). Chicago: Moody Press.
[9] Guzik, D. (2013). *Matthew* (Mt 5:3). Santa Barbara, CA: David Guzik.
[10] MacArthur, J. F., Jr. (1985). *Matthew* (p. 145). Chicago: Moody Press.
[11] Hughes, R. K. (2001). *The sermon on the mount: the message of the kingdom* (p. 19). Wheaton, IL: Crossway Books.
[12] Hughes, R. K. (2001). *The sermon on the mount: the message of the kingdom* (p. 22). Wheaton, IL: Crossway Books.
[13] Hughes, R. K. (2001). *The sermon on the mount: the message of the kingdom* (p. 19). Wheaton, IL: Crossway Books.
[14] Accessed 3/4/17 from http://www.christianitytoday.com/moi/2011/006/december/too-busy-not-to-pray.html
[15] Hughes, R. K. (2001). *The sermon on the mount: the message of the kingdom* (p. 30). Wheaton, IL: Crossway Books.
[16] Guzik, D. (2013). *Matthew* (Mt 5:4). Santa Barbara, CA: David Guzik.

[17] Stott, J. R. W. (1988). *The Letters of John: An Introduction and Commentary* (Vol. 19, p. 130). Downers Grove, IL: InterVarsity Press.
[18] Hughes, R. K. (2001). *The sermon on the mount: the message of the kingdom* (p. 30). Wheaton, IL: Crossway Books.
[19] Hughes, R. K. (2001). *The sermon on the mount: the message of the kingdom* (pp. 30–31). Wheaton, IL: Crossway Books.
[20] Hughes, R. K. (2001). *The sermon on the mount: the message of the kingdom* (p. 29). Wheaton, IL: Crossway Books.
[21] MacArthur, J. F., Jr. (1985). *Matthew* (p. 170). Chicago: Moody Press.
[22] Hughes, R. K. (2001). *The sermon on the mount: the message of the kingdom* (pp. 34–35). Wheaton, IL: Crossway Books.
[23] Barclay, W. (2001). *The Gospel of Matthew* (Third Ed., p. 111). Edinburgh: Saint Andrew Press.
[24] Barclay, W. (2001). *The Gospel of Matthew* (Third Ed., p. 111). Edinburgh: Saint Andrew Press.
[25] Hughes, R. K. (2001). *The sermon on the mount: the message of the kingdom* (pp. 37–38). Wheaton, IL: Crossway Books.
[26] Hughes, R. K. (2001). *The sermon on the mount: the message of the kingdom* (p. 36). Wheaton, IL: Crossway Books.
[27] Hughes, R. K. (2001). *The sermon on the mount: the message of the kingdom* (p. 37). Wheaton, IL: Crossway Books.
[28] Boice, J. M. (2002). *The Sermon on the Mount: an expositional commentary* (p. 41). Grand Rapids, MI: Baker Books.
[29] Boice, J. M. (2002). *The Sermon on the Mount: an expositional commentary* (p. 41). Grand Rapids, MI: Baker Books.
[30] MacArthur, J. F., Jr. (1985). *Matthew* (p. 181). Chicago: Moody Press.
[31] MacArthur, J. F., Jr. (1985). *Matthew* (p. 183). Chicago: Moody Press.
[32] MacArthur, J. F., Jr. (1985). *Matthew* (pp. 186–187). Chicago: Moody Press.
[33] MacArthur, J. F., Jr. (1985). *Matthew* (p. 190). Chicago: Moody Press.
[34] MacArthur, J. F., Jr. (1985). *Matthew* (p. 188). Chicago: Moody Press.
[35] Hughes, R. K. (2001). *The sermon on the mount: the message of the kingdom* (p. 49). Wheaton, IL: Crossway Books.
[36] MacArthur, J. F., Jr. (1985). *Matthew* (p. 202). Chicago: Moody Press.

[37] MacArthur, J. F., Jr. (1985). *Matthew* (p. 202). Chicago: Moody Press.
[38] Barclay, W. (2001). *The Gospel of Matthew* (Third Ed., p. 122). Edinburgh: Saint Andrew Press.
[39] MacArthur, J. F., Jr. (1985). *Matthew* (p. 204). Chicago: Moody Press.
[40] Boice, J. M. (2002). *The Sermon on the Mount: an expositional commentary* (p. 46). Grand Rapids, MI: Baker Books.
[41] MacArthur, J. F., Jr. (1985). *Matthew* (p. 211). Chicago: Moody Press.
[42] Carson, D. A. (1999). *Jesus' Sermon on the Mount and His Confrontation with the World: An Exposition of Matthew 5–10* (p. 28). Grand Rapids, MI: Baker Academic.
[43] Carson, D. A. (1999). *Jesus' Sermon on the Mount and His Confrontation with the World: An Exposition of Matthew 5–10* (p. 28). Grand Rapids, MI: Baker Academic.
[44] Barclay, W. (2001). *The Gospel of Matthew* (Third Ed., p. 126). Edinburgh: Saint Andrew Press.
[45] MacArthur, J. F., Jr. (1985). *Matthew* (p. 218). Chicago: Moody Press.
[46] Hughes, R. K. (2001). *The sermon on the mount: the message of the kingdom* (p. 66). Wheaton, IL: Crossway Books.
[47] MacArthur, J. F., Jr. (1985). *Matthew* (pp. 217–218). Chicago: Moody Press.
[48] Hughes, R. K. (2001). *The sermon on the mount: the message of the kingdom* (p. 72). Wheaton, IL: Crossway Books.
[49] Hughes, R. K. (2001). *The sermon on the mount: the message of the kingdom* (p. 73). Wheaton, IL: Crossway Books.
[50] MacArthur, J. F., Jr. (1985). *Matthew* (p. 222). Chicago: Moody Press.
[51] MacArthur, J. F., Jr. (1985). *Matthew* (p. 224). Chicago: Moody Press.
[52] Hughes, R. K. (2001). *The sermon on the mount: the message of the kingdom* (p. 73). Wheaton, IL: Crossway Books.
[53] Barclay, W. (2001). *The Gospel of Matthew* (Third Ed., pp. 128–129). Edinburgh: Saint Andrew Press.
[54] MacArthur, J. F., Jr. (1985). *Matthew* (p. 223). Chicago: Moody Press.
[55] MacArthur, J. F., Jr. (1985). *Matthew* (pp. 223–224). Chicago: Moody Press.

[56] Hughes, R. K. (2001). *The sermon on the mount: the message of the kingdom* (p. 70). Wheaton, IL: Crossway Books.

CPSIA information can be obtained
at www.ICGtesting.com
Printed in the USA
LVHW021444200721
693194LV00011B/1052

9 781548 498818